MW01059763

HIS

H I S

**A Single Girl's Journey to Discovering
God's Heart on Love, Marriage and Identity**

Alysha Miller

XULON PRESS

Xulon Press
2301 Lucien Way #415
Maitland, FL 32751
407.339.4217
www.xulonpress.com

Paperback ISBN-13: 978-1-6628-2242-1
Ebook ISBN-13: 978-1-6628-2243-8

This book is dedicated to the God who saved me.
Apart from Him, I can do nothing.

To Jesus, my forever Husband.

And to my two best friends—my brother, Aaron,
and my faithful (furry) sidekick, Lily.

My prayer for this book:

Lord,

Bring those
who are afar off, home.
Bring healing to our minds, bodies
and salvation to our souls.
Restore our families, marriages and hearts.
Teach us what it is to be Kingdom minded.

Ignite our spiritual lives.
Set us free from our own evil desires.
Revive the hearts of those
who read from these pages.
May the words fan a flame by
Your Holy Spirit's power.

Help us to see You.
And to desire You.
And to open ourselves up to You.

Save us from ourselves.
In Jesus' name, amen.

Contents

Then I saw a new heaven and a new earth, for the old heaven
and the old earth had disappeared.
And the sea was also gone.
And I saw the holy city, the new Jerusalem,
coming down from God out of heaven
like a bride beautifully dressed for her husband.
I heard a loud shout from the throne, saying,
"Look, God's home is now among his people!
He will live with them, and they will be his people.
God himself will be with them.
He will wipe every tear from their eyes,
and there will be no more death or sorrow or crying or pain.
All these things are gone forever.
And the one sitting on the throne said, "Look, I am making
everything new!"
And then he said to me, "Write this down, for what I tell you is
trustworthy and true."
And he also said, "It is finished! I am the Alpha and the Omega—
the Beginning and the End.
To all who are thirsty I will give freely from the springs of the
water of life.
All who are victorious will inherit all these blessings,
and I will be their God, and they will be my children.

— Revelation 21:1–7

Foreword

In the pages of *His*, you'll find Alysha's powerful testimony and see the amazing grace of God over her life and all He offers to you and me. Alysha is not only a trusted friend of mine but most importantly my sister in Christ. When we first connected over podcasting it became apparent that our broken pasts hinged on much of the same thing; hearts that sought validation, acceptance, and affirmation from the world. Through our friendship, I've seen firsthand her heart for girls and women of all ages to know God fully and experience Him in a way that transforms every facet of life.

Through the writing of *His*, Alysha takes you through not only her journey of redemption but she also shares what she walked through before knowing Him personally. While reading, she'll become a trusted friend or mentor. Throughout this book she makes you feel heard, seen, and understood. My favorite thing about this book is that it isn't written from the place of "I told you so", but written from the place of "I've walked here too." There is nothing better than reading a book where you know the writer has felt the pain of what you may be currently walking through.

Perhaps you're holding this book wondering what all the Lord has in store for you as you read *His*. I want you to know this, you will not be the same after you turn the last page. Jesus changes everything. Your heart will see the goodness of God and what He desires for you. You will hear truth in its purest form and those truths will start to pierce the hardened places of your heart.

Ephesians 5:11-14 came to mind as I was going through parts of this book, "Take no part in the unfruitful works of darkness, but instead expose them. For it is shameful even to speak of the things that they do in secret. But when anything is exposed by the light, it becomes visible, for anything that becomes visible is light. Therefore it says,"Awake, O sleeper, and arise from the dead, and Christ will shine on you." Alysha invites you to live this out. Her words ask you to bring before the light all unfruitful works of darkness. Each page might have you feeling like the darkness is being exposed but rest in this, through the dark parts being exposed, the light of Christ is shining through, redeeming and renewing you from the inside out.

The work of the Lord in your heart is a beautiful thing but often times painful when the pruning begins. As you read *His* you will see love spelled out in the way God always had intended; sourced from Him alone. This makes the pruning one of celebration. A victory knowing that old has passed and the new thing the Lord wants to do can begin happening. Most importantly, picture Jesus covering you and pointing you to a life renewed in Him because of who He is. Rejoice as you're met with conviction and trust in the testimony God is writing for you. He is good, He is faithful, and remember - you are His.

— Chelsey DeMatteis,
author of *More of Him Less of Me,
Living a Christ-Centered Life in a
Me-Centered World* and
podcast host of *Living with Less Podcast*

Introduction

When God moves, He moves. And not only does He move, He moves big! Moving in such a way, more times than not, causes me to audibly laugh and just simply breathe the word "Incredible." You might often hear Christians say, "It was such a God thing!" or "Only God!" and we really mean it. I could write an entire book on all the "only God" things I've encountered in the 8 years I've been walking with Him. Maybe I will one day. For now, this book is one of those "only God" things. I actually can't believe it.

You're holding a copy of *His: A Single Girl's Journey to Discovering God's Heart on Love, Marriage and Identity* in your hands—your one-of-a kind, uniquely gifted, wonderfully crafted hands. God made those hands of yours! Not only am I a writer but a photographer as well, and I had a friend tell me once, I focus a lot of my frames on people's hands. I never realized until those words came out of her mouth that that's true. Hands tell such a rich story, but what really matters is what our hands are capable of, especially when they're palm-faced up, open and surrendered.

This may sound really weird, but I feel truly honored that your hands picked up this book. I'm really imagining it. Who you are I may never know, but I can be sure it's not an accident you picked this book up. And I've prayed for you. Every copy of this book sent out has been prayed over. My prayer was specifically for the hands that will hold *this* book. Whether they are trembling hands, scarred hands, tattooed hands, unsure hands, crippled hands, I pray this book would be an extension of the Father's hands and heart to steady and ready yours for what He wants to build through your hands. Kingdom-purposed hands.

I pray if anyone reading this is handcuffed to their sin that this book and its core message, which is the gospel, will be the key to unlock what's keeping you bound to your sin or shame. There are many references to Scripture throughout this book; the Bible and its life-giving words is what truly sets us free. It's what breathed life back into my lifeless hands and has propelled me forward ever since. It's what makes me proudly declare "I am HIS!" and I'll tell you a little more about what that means throughout this book.

I pray as I share parts of my story that it will be a mirror in your hands, reflected back to see yourself and to see your sin plainly and to be broken over it. Brokenness is a gift. It places us rightly before a holy God, a forgiving God, a God whose hands extend out unmerited mercy to us. My prayer is that each person that reads this book will own their sin once they see it for what it is yet be freed from the shame the devil wants to attach to it. Jesus wouldn't want that. It would negate what He did on the cross for you. He bore your shame and your sin, and nails were driven through *His* hands to prove it (grab a Bible if you have one and read what John 20:20 says about that).

It's important to know we're spiritually sick and need healing. I think most people could agree with that but argue against Jesus being the only way to true healing because of political correctness or they want to keep living the way they're living, even though it's hurting them. Jesus said, "Healthy people don't need a doctor—sick people do" (Matt. 9:12, NLT) and then He added, "For I have come to call not those who think they are righteous, but those who know they are sinners" (Matt. 9:13, NLT). There is healing in acknowledging our sin and there is power in the name of Jesus, whose name blots it out. It's in Jesus's name alone that sin patterns break, captives are set free, and spiritual eyes are opened.

I'm truly in awe that God has given me the words and the diligence to write them down, type them all out, and have someone believe in the angle of this story so much so as to publish it. To have this in your hands means the Lord has protected the word document throughout the writing process and helped me through the printing and publishing feat that felt like a mountain climb. So often I read books and wonder how so many authors just pump books out. This was not so with this one. Maybe it's not so with others, either. But it's a praise report that you have this finished work completed in your hands.

What you hold are the broken pieces of my story or at least a piece of the journey to wholeness and healing on the way to glory (Heaven). These are some of the pieces of my story that have been restored and redeemed by my Royal Husband, which have been shaped into a book and into a project and podcast called *The Marriage Project*. This book is divided into three parts—"The Bride," the telling of my story; "The Project," the telling of how the vision for the project came about; and "The Bridegroom and The Wedding Feast," telling of who the Bridegroom is and what that means for eternity. The irony is that I began a marriage ministry, yet I am still not married. Brief summation: I was a hot mess express, and God had a lot to teach this once boy-crazed, party girl on the subject of who He is, and on marriage, men, and relationships. These pages hold the story of the road that led this once broken girl to discover God's heart on marriage, purity, and identity.

As we go a little deeper, I want to make sure you know the heart of this King, Jesus, who loves you so passionately and wholly. If ever there is a part you feel turned off while reading, then I say, "Good." My words are intended as arrows, not Band-aids. This culture of acceptance is damaging to true healing and growth. I'm simply being the person I wish I had at the time I needed to be called out. Sometimes truth hurts and it's necessary to pierce the hard parts of your heart to create a break, a crack so that light may shine through. There's the fair warning. Every part of this is typed coming from a girl who has been there before. I'm not the girl judging you. I'm the sister who has wept for you. The sister whose heart so desperately wants you to find peace promised by salvation from the Prince of Peace and who desires you to know purity in the midst of a contaminated, mixed-up world. The hardest part about writing for me is not being able to see your expression or you see mine. So imagine a smile and a warm heart sitting across from yours as you sit down to read. It's the love of Christ that swells up in my heart, and I can't help but pour it out in this way. I imagine these pages soaking, saturated in Jesus's love for you.

This introduction is to serve as an appetizer to the main course. The meat of this message is to share with you the love and joy and peace I have found in a vibrant, thriving relationship with the living God through Jesus Christ and the irony of Him leading this single girl who once idolized marriage and who once found her worth in relationships to create a project that shines God's heart for marriage and knowing Him as First Love.

I felt led to create a project that stands for the sanctity of marriage and to do so in testimony format because there is power in a testimony. I wanted to interview and ask Christian couples what they've discovered about God's heart and their own heart as they've been married and to turn it into a podcast with the aid of visual storytelling. The project's mission is to point out that marriage is the very portrait God uses to demonstrate His covenant love for His people and to display the Bride of Christ, which is what Jesus calls His church.

There's no denying the work God has done in so many different people from different walks of life and how their life changed when they accepted Jesus as their Lord and Savior. We are all testifying to the same God, the One True God, the Hebrew God of the Bible, and His miraculous, transformative work in our lives. I will share more about what a testimony even is and get into what exactly this project, The Marriage Project, is in the pages to come.

So how do we get to all of that? Where do we begin? Let's begin with a girl and the first "only God" thing He did in me—radically transforming this rebel from the inside out. I will tell how the Fiery Flame of His holy love began to burn inside my heart and how the Vine Dresser pruned, prodded, and extracted vile things from my heart and mind. And oh how it hurt—but oh, how I needed it. I know it's all for my ultimate good. It's readying me for that day I will come face to face with my Maker, my Redeemer, the Bridegroom, Jesus Christ. "As a young man marries a young woman, so will your Builder marry you; as a bridegroom rejoices over his bride, so will your God rejoice over you" (Isa. 62:5, NLT).

As this goes for me, the same goes for you. Whether you know Jesus or not, by the end of this I pray you feel more closely acquainted with Him and more than that, that you find yourself madly in love with the One who has always loved you. He gave His life for you to save you from your sin and eternal death. I pray that He would do a work in your life and graciously lead you to believe in Him so that your love for Him will burst and cause you to want to shake this culture up by doing life, relationships, and marriage His way. And that He will help you in understanding that He is coming back for His church, His bride soon and to think soberly on this truth. It's prophesied in the Bible. Everything else the Bible predicted before has been fulfilled. This is next on the prophetic calendar, Jesus returning.

Will our hearts be ready? Do we even know what that means?

Part 1—The Bride

1

To Have, To Hold, and To Let Go

"Behold, I am doing a new thing; now it springs forth,
do you not perceive it?
I will make a way in the wilderness and rivers in the desert."
— Isaiah 43:19

I never had aspirations of being a career woman, let alone a business owner. Becoming an author could have been the more realistic dream, I suppose, as I have always loved to read and write, but even that wasn't a goal of mine. Yet here I stand at age 32 with a wedding photography business and Lord willing, a book published. To call me into the wedding industry is God's way of showing off His sense of humor because the dream of mine growing up was to be a wife. I idolized marriage and having the perfect relationship all throughout my young adult/teen years and well into my early twenties.

A collection of Barbie dolls filled my room when I was growing up. I remember having to leave them "mid-play" when school or homework interrupted. As I said, I was always a reader and loved making up stories for my dolls. I'd rush home from school and try to get my homework done as quickly as possible so that I could get back to where the story of my Barbies left off. It never failed, I would work a wedding into most of the stories. I wonder how many times my Barbie and Ken dolls actually got married to each other. Barbie would put on her Velcro-backed wedding gown, her veil, and plastic white shoes and walk slowly down the aisle to her "happily ever after." Sealed with a kiss, of course.

Death of A Dream

The innate desire for intimacy and marriage was embedded in my being even from an early age. Is that the way it is for all of us? Maybe not all, but I would guess most of us. I let myself believe that I would one day be the bride with the dress and would have the happily ever after too. Having been a dreamer and a writer, it wasn't hard for me to dream up a story about the perfect romance or relationship. I had allowed my mind to be filled with thoughts of an idyllic relationship for a lot of my formative to teenage years. The problem was that a lot of the storylines derived from where I was looking: the movies and the magazines. I can't even imagine where my mind would have gone if social media had been a thing, but thankfully back then it wasn't. These superficial influences didn't help mute my natural whimsical tendencies. It bolstered them. Hollywood always projected that lie of perfection. So that's what I assumed would be the story, *my* story, and I'd write the narrative and script in my mind and play it out over and over. I let my thought life get the best of me.

It's a great desire to have—to be happily married and deeply in love with your spouse—but there was so much error in my way of thinking. I wasn't thinking about it from a biblical perspective or thinking about the way God designed marriage. I didn't even know what that meant. And I didn't realize this then, but it was incredibly unfair to put that sort of pressure or expectation on my future spouse. A spouse wasn't intended to fulfill me entirely or at all. Plus, no spouse would ever be perfect. I needed to let that dream die.

While the harm wasn't in the dream itself, it was in how much importance I placed on that thing to define me and bring about my happiness. It was the one goal to attain, and if I didn't get it, I couldn't be happy. I realized later my desire stemmed from my need to be validated and affirmed through a relationship. Validation, acceptance, and affirmation were the things I began making idols out of. I wanted someone to just *see* me and choose me so desperately. The real chains that held me captive in my mind were insecurity, comparison, and that ideal of perfection. When Jesus got ahold of my heart, I came to realize I needed to accept the brokenness of people and let the dream of a "perfect" anything die. Except for Him. Only He is perfect, and only He can offer a love that satisfies.

I couldn't find my security in an insecure world. I needed to find it in a secure God. As much as marriage might bring some sort of periodic happiness, I've discovered God created marriage to bring about holiness in us, not happiness. Yet I was never told that. Pop culture doesn't believe that, know that, and would never tell you that. They wouldn't tell me marriage, sex, and human love weren't meant to fulfill me. That wouldn't sell. In this life we are all searching for meaning and purpose. The world will tell you the ultimate purpose in life is to find happiness. We're taught to think it can be found in another finite being, a human. We're also taught to think love is the ultimate goal and once we find it, we'll have found true meaning and belonging. That's true. However, we were made for an otherworldly, supernatural love, God's love. Human love will always come up short, no matter what. People will fail us. It's usually when the facade of passion wears off, we realize they're not the missing puzzle piece to happiness after all.

So we keep searching—or numbing ourselves. My friend recently told me a story of her Uber driver who was divulging a bit too much of his personal life and told her he had two failed marriages. His reasoning? He "just didn't know how to pick 'em." I thought, "It's not about picking but about sticking" and sticking to that commitment regardless of fizzled fuzzy feelings. It sounds like he decided to leave because he thought he hadn't met his match yet, that because he wasn't happy he had chosen wrong. That's not it at all but that's what we have been taught to believe, that it's all about finding "the one." The false thinking is that "clearly if they're not making us happy anymore, they weren't the one."

As a once hopeless romantic, I bought into that as well, although now I see it differently. There *is* One[1] our hearts were made for, but that love is not found in a flesh-and-blood type of relationship we might imagine. It's found in a flesh-and-blood relationship with Jesus, the One who gave up His life for the sin of mankind. It was *His* flesh that paid for our freedom, dying for our sin, which condemned us to death, being born "dead in sin."[2] It was by *His* blood, spilled out for us by His death on the cross. It's actually a relief to discover that the hole in our heart is a Jesus-sized hole. Anything else that tries to fit in His place won't. Because God created us for Himself. It's the answer we've all been looking for. Any hopelessness caused by romance can be replaced with hopefulness found in Him.

That is our meaning and purpose in this life. We were created by the Creator to share in His glory and His perfection and will get to experience the wonder of Heaven with every other believer for all eternity, while getting glimpses of that glory now. To be quite

---

[1] Any words capitalized like "one" or "Prince of Peace" is to signify Christ's deity and titles. Where there is capitalization of a title, I am referring to Jesus Christ.

[2] Reference to the English Translation Version of the Bible, the one I recommend in the Author's Note.

honest, all of what I just wrote never used to appeal to me or make any sense. My flesh rejected it. My evil heart denied Christ and His love. I wish I could say it's because I didn't know the immensity of His love and what Heaven would truly be like and what eternity separated from Him would really feel like. In reality, my sin kept me separated from God and I was fine with that. I liked my sin. It truly is by grace that we are saved (Eph. 2:8–9).

Anything good comes from God, and we fail to recognize it is *our* sin that separates us from Him. We can't live in sin and have God too. He's too holy, too just. The good news is (this is the gospel) that Jesus came as the lifeline, through that flesh-and-blood sacrifice to pay for the deeds of my flesh and its sin-driven tendencies and the blood that's on my hands. In that sacrifice we find forgiveness of sin and have our relationship with God restored through Christ, and that gives us the great privilege of calling Him Father.

To stay on this just a little longer, I share this next part with you in hopes that it would cause you to desire the things of Heaven and of God more. To dream about not just the "one day" here on earth but to think beyond it into eternity and where you'll spend it. Heaven won't be boring contrary to what popular culture will tell you. It will be every "good" thing this earth offers. I put quotes around "good" because "good" can become easily misconstrued. "Good" is defined here as the purest of things, which make our hearts swell with joy—heartfelt community, hot bread/meals with our loved ones, neighbors serving neighbors, the beauty of earth's natural wonders, to name a few. Now imagine that perfected with no contention, jealousy, backstabbing, lust, adultery, greed, murder, impure motives, malice, bad tempers, or impatient spirits. Then add the beauty of this world without the carnage of pollution, sewage, and landfills, no telephone wires distracting from the night's painted sunset sky and the best part—His presence dwelling rightly among us. His presence made known in full.

Andrew Murray wrote, "When God created the universe, it was with the objective of making those He created partakers of His perfection and blessedness, thus showing forth the glory of His love and wisdom and power. God desired to reveal Himself in and through His creatures by communicating to them as much of His own goodness and glory as they were capable of receiving. But this communication was not meant to give created beings something they could possess in themselves, having full charge and access apart from Him. Rather, God as the ever-living, ever-present, ever-acting One, who upholds all things by the word of His power and in whom all things exist, meant that the relationship of His creatures to Himself would be one of unceasing, absolute dependence."[3]

It was God's intended plan to have us be partakers in His perfection and blessedness. We get to experience all the truly good things in their perfected states one day in Heaven. The alternative to this is hell for eternity: "They will be punished with everlasting destruction and shut out from the presence of the Lord and from the glory of his might" (2 Thessalonians 1:9, NIV). He wants that for no one and gives many warnings and extends many opportunities to receive Christ and be reconciled to Him before that final fate is sealed.

Because of sin entering and contaminating the world, we are unable to experience real love or any restored, new thing apart from Him. So all those contaminated messages Hollywood sold me as a young girl? He had to break through many years of negative influences,

---

[3] Andrew Murray was a South African writer, teacher and Christian pastor. This little book titled, Humility, is one we should keep in our pockets for reference throughout the day. Its size and the truths packed in are applicable for everyday life (outside of the Bible) and I know I need these reminders constantly.

a misinformed, stubborn mindset, and He patiently worked at removing the death grip I had on attaining that "perfect" relationship.

This idyllic thought life I entertained wasn't just reserved for daydreaming about relationships. I would catch myself dreaming of faraway places and romanticizing them in my mind. This continued into my adult life as well. I learned a lesson in this later on as God was revealing things to me after I had surrendered my life and thought life over to Him.

The Year Was 2013

When the opportunity to go to Paris came, I began dreaming like I'd been accustomed to. I imagined cobblestone, pristine streets lined with balloons floating through the air, and I let that consume my thoughts over practicality. How quickly that bubble was burst when I stepped foot off the plane into reality and into the 18th arrondissement known as the Montmartre district of Paris. What I saw were streets muddied and the gutters littered with trash and human waste. I wasn't a stranger to the ruder and cruder things at this point in my life; I'd been living that way for quite some time, but the street signs and atmosphere in the Moulin Rouge side of town were even a bit much for me.

This was Paris? As much as I sulked in the discomfort and unfamiliarity of it all for the first few days, I started to see there was a resiliency about this city and despite the spiritually dark climate, God was redefining beauty for me. This was around the time He was starting to really soften my heart to Him. He keyed me into the architecture, the accents, the cafes, the art, colors—and the Italian gelato. The French croissants and macaroons, too. I had to acclimate to the harsher reality to fully appreciate the parts that shone through. It was the city's grit, as well as the broken and the reviled parts of the entire experience that made the other parts shine that much more brilliantly. While I was walking through it, I had to loosen the grip my whimsical heart craved and embrace Paris for all it was if I were to enjoy any parts of it. I imagine God prying my white knuckled fingers off unrealistic dream after unrealistic dream, one by one.

I'm so glad He did. I'm so glad my story hasn't gone my way or the way the movies told me it should go. The script to the story I was dreaming up doesn't hold a candle to the stories God writes. Because His stories for us are His story. We're merely grafted in to a much larger story, a story of redemption. His stories build a resiliency in a weak creature (man) through loving mercy. The hard parts we walk through, the unattractive middle, is producing something far greater than any fairytale or turbulent Hollywood ending ever could.

In Paris, I had a choice—to write the whole city off or laugh through the unexpected hurdles, the unprepared for mishaps and journal about it anyway. After all, that was the story. That's the lesson I was learning. The dream I dreamed was not. Funnily enough, there is a nostalgic charm when I think back to it all. Gratitude has since been cultivated in my heart. It really was wonderful, and I haven't quite experienced anything like it. But first, I needed to learn to appreciate the broken as well as the beauty. I needed to let go of any preconceived notions I had and appreciate it at face value. If I could do that, I'd be on to something. I've learned to take that same lesson and apply it to life and to relationships. I have to let go of my expectations and hold reality up to the truth of God's Word and what He says about the very thing I'm fantasizing about in my mind.

It can be heartbreaking to confront the truth of something, yet it forces us to come to terms with reality, and we must drop the pretenses we may have bought into because of influences of shows or highlight reels on social media we've allowed into our lives. To confront the truth about the brokenness of human nature and the sin in us has caused me to hold fast to my convictions and let the truth of God's Word be my only compass. It has also caused me to become more empathetic instead of apathetic, stopping to look the brokenness of humanity in the eyes because humanity is made in God's image just as much as I am. Before God entered my heart, I couldn't care less about any of that. I was so fixated on myself and my dreams that I couldn't see past either.

The reality is facing the darker parts of the human heart and the inevitable truth that we are sinners and that we all have fallen short of the glory of God (Romans 3:23). The reality is knowing that my relationships or a marriage aren't going to be perfect this side of Heaven because of sin. But it brings peace knowing that we can count on Jesus, who is without sin, and life, relationships, and marriage centered on Him will be made better, richer, and fuller. He knows how to work with the cracks, the broken pieces, and the rough edges of this world because He is God and He came down to live in it, among His people.

Since giving my life to Christ, I've been on one really intense rollercoaster with my desire for and dreams of marriage. Did I ever imagine being single this long when I first gave my life to Christ? (We're talking going on 8 years of singleness, as in not having a clearly defined relationship.) Definitely not! If I had known that years of singleness was part of God's plan for my life, I might have been more hesitant about the plan because all I wanted was *my* plan, which was to be in a relationship. You know, the Velcro-backed Barbie wedding dress and plastic shoes plan? I wanted a wedding. But that's why He doesn't show us the entirety of His plan for our lives from the get-go. It's a step by step, day by day walking out His plan for your life.

There have been seasons in my life where the longing for a companion was almost too much to bear. Then there were the times where the dream of one day being married sounded like the least appealing thing in my mind. I've had moments where I've had to squeeze every heart pang out in prayer because I couldn't take the waiting any longer. Then there have been the moments I'm so content in where the Lord has me that I think I'd be okay if it never did work out the way I always dreamed it would. He is good that way. No matter what the outcome, I'll always be His. Singleness really is a gift because we can be fully devoted to God with uninterrupted time spent with Him. We can really discover who He's calling us to be with zero inhibitions.

I've also come to learn in this time of letting go and the "confronting reality season" that anything worth having or anything great doesn't come easy or especially fast. In a race, crossing the finish line feels so validating because of the training, prepping, and determination to reach the goal. I imagine waiting on this piece of the story, a God-breathed relationship and marriage (if that's His plan for me, for you) will be as rewarding as that running through the ribbon at a finish line.

As God had begun transforming me from crudeness to a new creation in Christ, my new dream became being God's daughter and growing in love with Him first. If in time, marriage and being a wife comes, I only want it God's way. I've also learned that our race doesn't begin when marriage does. I always thought that way. But now, I understand it begins way before. We are not defined by who we're dating or if we are or aren't married. We may be in the training period, where character is being matured to endure the stretch that is marriage, but I believe as we begin to run, if God's will for your life is marriage, a spouse will come running right alongside you when the time is right. I'm confident doing marriage God's way will bring more of that endurance building. Sure, it will strengthen a muscle only marriage can. Yet God uses our singleness and other things to strengthen us all the same.

For far too long, I believed that I wouldn't be happy until I was married or that I could create my own happiness and force my own dream to come true in relationships, but in doing so I rejected God and His great love for me. The scary part is when we do leave God out of our lives, that broken reality, the muddied gutters and littered streets, becomes the "dream" that comes true. Without God at the center of something it will all eventually come to a screeching halt as our sin natures collide and everything we've worked toward achieving is nothing but dust. What are you left with?

A New Dream

So, unlike my Barbie brides, I haven't been the bride yet, but I'm okay with that. And until then, I get to live in a world with real brides that keeps me quite familiar with all things wedding related because of the ministry and work God has called me to. You see, brides have been written into my story all along. The beginning of my walk with Jesus started with a new dream, new desires, which were all given by Him, because remember my dreams and desires? Very nearsighted. Before God led me to begin a wedding photography business, the Lord began to renew my thought life, and I saw a new image, it was the image of a bride—from the dress to the veil and her ethereal beauty—to illustrate to me who the Bride really is and that we as Christ followers can all be a part of this identity. The Bride is Christ's bride, His Church. He defines His Church as His bride. What that means is, "Just as there was a betrothal period in biblical times during which the bride and groom were separated until the wedding, so is the bride of Christ separate from her Bridegroom during the church age." It is the answer to that last question posed in the introduction. We, as Christ's Church, are waiting for His return. He has promised to come again to reign on a new Earth, one that will be even better than my whimsical mind can conjure up.

On a personal level, I can now see myself in this same light because of what Jesus did for me. Adorned, radiant, redeemed. A bride. But I couldn't see this while I lived like a pauper, stuck in sin and stuck on a dead-end dream. I couldn't see. I was blind to the things in the spiritual realm. The world had chewed me up, and it didn't spit me out like the cliché says. It would have gladly kept me hadn't He in His grace come to my rescue. After all my deliberate disobedience, it was amazing to me that God still saw me this way— this imagery of a pure bride dressed in white, pure and blameless. In Christ, we are made pure, spotless, and blameless. He saw me this way because He knew I would be Christ's, who is as pure and as white as the whitest white dress. Sin's stain to be forever blotted out.

"...it is time to wake up to reality.
Every day brings God's salvation nearer.
The night is nearly over, the day has almost dawned.
Let us therefore fling away the things that men do in the dark,
let us arm ourselves for the fight of the day!
Let us live cleanly, as in the daylight,
not in the "delights" of getting drunk or playing with sex,
nor yet in quarreling or jealousies.
Let us be Christ's men from head to foot,
and give no chances to the flesh to have its fling."

— Romans 13:11–14

2

The Dress and The Road

"Who is this coming up from the wilderness
leaning on her beloved?"
— Song of Solomon 8:5

T he wedding dress? God's idea. God not only created gardens but garments as well. Fashion is strewn all about the Bible, and there's a specific verse tailored to wedding attire. "I am overwhelmed with joy in the LORD my God! For he has dressed me with the clothing of salvation and draped me in a robe of righteousness. I am like a bridegroom in his wedding suit or a bride with her jewels" (Isa. 61:10, NLT).

God has fashioned us and has sewn us into the fabric of the story of creation and redemption through Christ Jesus, and it's told throughout the entire Bible. Each one of us, scars and scar tissue included, who believe in Him is woven together, tightly knit into the promise of the inheritance given to Abraham's descendants. That verse from Isaiah is a proclamation, a shout of overwhelming joy because of the promise to those who receive salvation and sonship through belief in Him. We are also promised to be arrayed in fine linen, or like a bride adorned in jewels. My everyday attire right now is pretty plain. I can walk into a designer fashion store that sells the most beautiful things but proceed to walk out empty-handed because I cannot justify spending that kind of money on an item of clothing. But it doesn't take away from the jaw-dropping, stunning quality of some of those custom-made pieces. And these are garments made by human hands. Imagine—what might such fine linen look and feel like when the Lord dresses us? Will it be dripping with colors our eyes have never even seen and ornate texture? Will it be intricately detailed, beaded? Or will it be a pure white like the white wedding dress? Or possibly all of the above! But no matter, whatever garments we wear on the outside won't be nearly as important as what will have taken place inwardly—the spotless, blameless purification made complete as we are in Christ and as we reside with Him (Phil. 1:6).

As Christ Loves the Church

While Isaiah 61 makes mention of bridal attire, Ephesians 5 is the chapter in which the apostle Paul addresses husbands and calls them to love their wives as Christ loves His Church and gave himself for her. "He gave up his life for her to make her holy and clean, washed by the cleansing of God's word. He did this to present her to himself as a glorious church without a spot or wrinkle or any other blemish. Instead, she will be holy and without fault" (Eph. 5:26–27, NLT).

There are many mentions of weddings, marriage, a great wedding feast, a bridegroom, and bridal references in the Bible. Marriage is holy. This specific Ephesians verse is speaking directly to husbands. It's commanding them to give up their life for their wives to make them holy and clean. What a tremendous calling. Is that something we see every day? Probably not. A man must first have this perspective and to fear God enough to desire to take this calling seriously and to live it out. As women we should desire to wait for a man who will see to it that we be more radiant before the Father when we enter Heaven because of how they lived this calling out while keeping in mind, nobody will live this out perfectly. But it's okay to desire this quality in a husband, someone who will read God's Word and apply it to his life. Someone who will pray for you and love you sacrificially like Jesus demonstrated by giving up His life for you. I had grown so callous to the idea of men and marriage in my own life that I didn't believe men like that existed. I actually didn't even desire a man like that before God entered my heart and life. I would have scoffed at reading something like that, and maybe you just did too. Or maybe you're having a hard time believing someone like that exists, but through this project, God showed me they do. They're sinners who have been saved too.

One other thing stood out to me in those Ephesians verses. Does anyone like to iron or steam their clothes? I'm not a fan of ironing. I'd like to point out that it says we will be without spot or wrinkle. Think about that. No more ironing or steaming—we will forever be without any wrinkles or blemishes (now you can check my theology on that, I know this is a metaphor, but I can't imagine there being wrinkles in Heaven). He will iron out every crease. What's amazing to me is how our stories all bundled together, wrapped into one large tapestry of His redemption can one day be laid out with no wrinkles. Nothing out of order or out of line. Miraculous! And it's because He is holy, and He is God, and He can do all things.

Like I mentioned, Heaven won't be boring. We will be dressed in our heavenly garments, coming together as one body, one church to worship the God of the Universe in paradise. At the wedding feast of the Lamb, you will wear fine linen woven from the threads of every righteous act you did while waiting for the Bridegroom (Rev. 19:8). There it is: a promise and a challenge. That hits home a little more. How we wait matters. A majority of any person's life consists of waiting. This verse is proof that our life matters, and how we spend it matters too. It might be tempting to spend it frivolously, but living a life bringing honor and glory to God won't be for nothing. Our acts while we live and operate on this decrepit planet will amount to the thread count of our heavenly garments. Wow, that's a lot to take in.

Off Roading

So what about the dress and a road? The year 2013 was when I rededicated my life to Jesus and was truly saved. I had grown up in church, but I didn't know Jesus personally. I only knew the cartoon pictures of a man in a white robe feeding fish to a crowd from my Bible lessons I'd take home with me. But 2013 was different. It was the first time I grasped the weight of my sin and what it cost Him. It was the first time I called him Lord. And it was the first time I realized it wasn't just nails that held Jesus to that cross, it was His unfailing love. And more specifically, His unfailing love for me.

This is where my story—or the story of being reborn—begins. This is where He began to restore me and gave me sight to see things I had never seen before: (1) I saw sin for what it was, (2) I saw a clear distinction of where I'd been, and (3) I saw where we (Jesus and I) were headed. I began to see past the temporal things luring me in and had a new vision in place where those fantasies once dwelled. With this new perspective, I had a vision. In it, I had on a white dress. I envisioned that even as a young girl, I had it on, and I was twirling around in this simple, white dress. However, my little defiant spirit came out time and again and would begin to soil it. The Bible tells us we are born into sin, "Behold, I was brought forth in iniquity, and in sin my mother did conceive me" (Ps. 51:5, ESV). I never had to be taught the words "mine" (selfish) or "no" (rebellious). You're never too young to begin sinning, it's just in our DNA, and it shouldn't be controversial or offensive to say that. It just is what it is.

As I grew up, I imagine there'd be a few more metaphorical grass stains while playing in this white, twirly metaphorical dress and of course the stains from some talkbacks and stubborn moods mixed in too. If it isn't apparent, in this vision sin was staining the pure whiteness this white dress symbolized. Then at age 13, I begged my mom to let me wear makeup. I threw tantrums when she would not let me go to the movies where I might run into my crush and have a little eye contact because I was too afraid to go talk to him. Fast forward to age 15, a time that I found myself in a relationship with a guy I really liked and where my innocence was lost, or rather was stolen, and the dress suddenly had a rip at the shoulder seam. After years of feeding my mind with mixed-up Hollywood messages, dreaming romantic dreams, listening to crude rap, I found myself in a tempting situation with my boyfriend, and I had suddenly been exposed to things I'd never seen or done before, and the purity I'd had as that young twirling girl was no more. I was worried about things I'd never had to worry about, and I was confused. I liked this person, but why hadn't he treated me with honor and respect? Why did he expect me to do things I wasn't comfortable doing? Did I have to do those things to keep him around? I liked having him around.

At this point in the vision, the sleeve of this dress was sloppily falling off the shoulder where it had torn. It was now just a dress on a lost girl, on a road going nowhere, like Cinderella after her stepsisters rip her dress to shreds with their insults and taunts. The road on the way to the light was filled with many dark days. During this time, my freshman high school year, I lost the sense of my worth and believed the harmful words that this guy I liked said to me. He said these things to my face, there was no mincing words. He jeered, mocked, and teased, poked and probed, name-called and coaxed. I took what he said about me as true because I already lacked self-confidence. I couldn't understand how someone could be so cruel just to be cruel. It only got worse, and all I wanted was to prove I was better than the names he was calling me.

I let this consume my every thought and emotion. I had to earn his affection, I wanted to prove what I was worth. I had unintentionally allowed a broken person driven by his sin nature to devalue me, and in doing so I began to sink. I quickly forgot what made that little girl laugh and smile. I sealed up any uncool parts of me (the parts that made me, me) and traded them in for cool. The problem with this decreasing self-worth was that it reflected in the treatment I was willing to accept. Any degrading thing any guy said about me was what I began to let define me. I no longer knew who I was. I wanted to be whoever this person I let manipulate me wanted me to be. The problem with an ever-changing identity is you will never be settled. It gets you tossed to and fro, having the same effect as sea sickness. I'd say it was in 6th grade that this attack on my identity began where I questioned everything. The boys I had crushes on asked other girls out, and I felt looked over. In junior high, my clothes were what brought the attention I desired. I had a handful of Saturday schools because my shorts were just a tad too short or because my shirt showed some of my midriff. I guess I thought looking a certain way might increase my chances at attaining the ultimate goal I had—being seen, being chosen, being loved...I will add our public school's dress code was a tad strict.

Although I was raised in a Christian home, the Bible was just another book to me, and God was just a subject talked about on Sundays when we'd go to church. The world around me felt more and more like "home" because it's what I was consuming the most of. I threw my Bible aside and turned on my radio, which only reaffirmed degrading messages said about women and our worth. The message coming through the speakers were nowhere near the cleansing call Ephesians 5 commands. And sadly, I was subscribed to the wrong message and listening to the wrong voices. "And what do you benefit if you gain the whole world but lose your own soul? Is anything worth more than your soul?" (Mrk. 8:36–37, NLT).

The answer is no, nothing is worth more than your soul, and Jesus and His death proves that. I soon found that I had in fact sold my soul for something I had been dreaming of since my Barbie and Ken playdates. What I bargained for, attention, affection, affirmation, ended up being counterfeit—counterfeit love, counterfeit affection, zero affirmation. It was all an illusion and all false. It was impossible for this mean-spirited person to give what I'd always hoped he'd give back. Yet he gave some sort of attention. He gave a tiny sliver of everything I thought I wanted, so I latched on. The attention was short-lived and became negative attention. I missed my friends who I'd stopped spending time with to spend time with this guy. Yet there would be another after him, one that was worse, which I couldn't have ever fathomed. I felt powerless against the manipulation, verbal abuse, and mind games. The sin nature. Both of ours feeding off the other's and creating a web I became more and more entangled in. I was isolated, frustrated, sad, and obsessed.

With all of that came this feeling of unworthiness. I began to sleepwalk through life and sleep around for a total of 9 years. Sexual sin is damaging to one's soul. God's heart grieves for the one trapped in its lure. I wasn't talking to God much during this time in my life, but I remember one specific instance where I was very aware of His presence in a pitch-black room, lying next to someone, and a tear fell from my eye. It wasn't my tear, I wasn't crying. An image of Jesus came into my thoughts, and I felt as if a tear had fallen out of His eye. *"Why are you doing this?"* This thought felt out of place, as negative thoughts seemed to be clouding my mind. My behavior made it hard to believe I'd ever be worthy of a kind, gentle, and devoted love, and it became even harder to keep believing for a white, wedding dress. I was no longer on any road, I had drifted far, far out to sea, far from the safety of the shore.

Freedom in Christ or Slave to Sin

The shore was my childhood and the security of my family's opinion and love for me. Yet not even that was enough to fill me. The thing is that the whole time God saw me and found me lovely. He believed I was worthy of the white dress, the one He had placed on me from the day I was born. But I was too busy to let Him in. I was too selfish to think about anyone but myself. I would learn the kindness and faithfulness of God and come back to the shoreline, but I had to swim through churning waters and would sink first. I had to come to the end of myself.

What do churning waters look like? Like I mentioned, abusive words that I still remember. Tolerating manipulative, possessive behavior from those two separate individuals over a span of 5 of the 9 aforementioned years. Both were overly jealous and treated me like an object, their object. I want to pause here and acknowledge you, the one still reading, still holding this book. If any person has made you to feel like you owe them something or have made you feel looked over, not chosen or unworthy, I am so sorry. I am so, so very sorry.

After I finally had the courage to leave the longer of these two relationships, a three-year drinking binge ensued. I felt I'd celebrate this newfound "freedom" with celebratory rounds of drinks, but again, these were more counterfeit offers, this was counterfeit freedom. This counterfeit freedom led to many more irresponsible decisions and expensive repercussions. I woke up with bruises from a bar fight I'd been pulled into (and don't really remember apart from the bruises), I'd scraped my knee falling off a curb because I was so drunk. It wasn't a pretty sight. While I was out of those prison-like abusive relationships, no chains had really been broken. I had become a slave to my sin, it just took on different forms. There is a chapter in the Bible specifically about freedom in Christ and life by the Spirit and compares it to the works of the flesh. Galatians 5:19–21 says this, "The acts of the flesh are obvious: sexual immorality, impurity and debauchery; idolatry and witchcraft; hatred, discord, jealousy, fits of rage, selfish ambition, dissensions, factions and envy; drunkenness, orgies, and the like. I warn you, as I did before, that those who live like this will not inherit the kingdom of God." When I first read those words, they were like salt in a wound; however, salt in a wound makes it heal faster.

Comparatively speaking, when we connect with God and abide in Him (John 15:5), He begins to produce in us spiritual fruit. This is something we're incapable of producing on our own. Soak in Jesus's words here as He explains this, "But the fruit of the Spirit [the result of His presence within us] is love [unselfish concern for others], joy, [inner] peace, patience [not the ability to wait, but how we act while waiting], kindness, goodness, faithfulness, gentleness, self-control. Against such things there is no law" (Gal. 5:22–23, AMP). It was so evident when I read these words years later that as I held my life up against Scripture, I was being led completely by my flesh, having no idea what it even meant to be led by the Spirit.

Another chapter that would become liberating is Romans 6 because it's an honest, abrupt, in your face reality check. "Don't you know that when you offer yourselves to someone as obedient slaves, you are slaves of the one you obey—whether you are slaves to sin, which leads to death, or to obedience, which leads to righteousness? But thanks be to God that, though you used to be slaves to sin, you have come to obey from your heart the pattern of teaching that has now claimed your allegiance. You have been set free from sin and have become slaves to righteousness" (Rom. 6:16–18, NIV).

Again, I was a slave to my sin because it's what I obeyed. I could not deny my flesh and continually indulged in behavior that wasn't pleasing to God. The way I was living was riddled with all that Galatians 5 listed out: sexual immorality, debauchery, drunkenness. Remember in our intro, the "hot mess express"? Here it was, and here I was. The most devastating part was my sin separated me from God. I couldn't be made right with Him until I repented, and I wouldn't let Him close enough to help me deal with any of it. I swept it all under a rug and reasoned that I'd deal with it later.

I had no idea how to truly get out of this mess I had made. These churning waters kept on churning. Did I even want out? Our hearts become hard when we don't surrender our pride. There were other ways to have fun, and there was a different way to live—in purity. I didn't need to let promiscuity rule me. I didn't think through the consequences and that every time I attached myself to another guy in that way, my soul was being tied to him. I hadn't yet learned that you do not have to give your body up to win affection or approval. It is not the commodity that you trade in for love. If that's what another person makes you feel you have to use as a transaction for their time and attention, it's definitely not love. And while celibacy might be an outdated word and may be countercultural and hard to pursue, the fight to stay pure might be easier than having to break a soul tie with a person you find yourself in bondage to.

Coming Up From the Wilderness

The most devastating part of being slave to sin was realizing everything I did on impulse has repercussions. Overdue credit card payments, missing work, walking out into broad daylight with last night's makeup smeared with a promise of him texting you later and hearing nothing. In this indulgent habit of having sex outside of marriage, I was taking away from what was really intended for my husband and giving it to someone who wasted much of my time and energy and exhausted my trust. Nothing ravages quite like sexual sin. It's unfortunate and could have been avoided, but it happened—bad boyfriends, hookups, toxic, abusive relationships. The dirt of this past accrued on my slanted, ripped, soiled dress. But in grace, the Lord has shown me that what I did in those 9 years does not define me. I'm made new in Christ (2 Cor. 5:17). That is my identity. Our sexuality or behavior is not our identity.

The thing to know is that the world and our sin are but two things that seek to come against us, but there is a third opponent. There is also this "d" word, the devil. Something I know now was that all of this was a distraction and a technique of the enemy. He is a thief. The Bible describes him as the chief thief "who comes to steal, kill and destroy" (Jn. 10:10). He comes to steal joy, goodness, purity, hope, perfect love, and our peace. He wanted me blind so that I'd stay in my sin, and that way I would stay separated from God who held the key to what I was looking for—pure, undefiled love. The good news is that while the thief comes to destroy, Jesus comes to give life abundant and give it to the full (Jn. 10:10). God is more powerful than the lying serpent. Relentless and redeeming, God's heart beats louder than a counterfeit anything. It is a steady, confident beat vs. a screeching, yelling, accusing beat.

The devil had certainly stirred the pot and the waters and caused many a shipwreck in my journey out at sea. There I was, trying to swim against the current that had become my life, but I could only fight from my own strength for so long. It finally got to a point where I could resist no longer. I was tired. The upkeep of the image of perfection? Exhausting. Five long years of accepting name-callings and pretending not to care when all I really did was care? Heavy. Four years of hangovers and casual hookups? Debilitating. And the heaviness became like weights around my ankles pulling me deeper and deeper into the dark abyss of my decisions. I wrote of running a race to build endurance and character; well, let me share this verse: "Therefore, since we are surrounded by such a huge crowd of witnesses to the life of faith, let us strip off every weight that slows us down, especially the sin that so easily trips us up. And let us run with endurance the race God has set before us" (Rom. 12:1, NLT).

I was nowhere near the finish line. I hadn't even started running the faith race. How could I? Sin was the weight tripping me up, pulling me down. If anything, I was panting on the sidelines of life. Try it one time. Throw some ten-pound weight bags on each of your legs next time you're on the treadmill or out for a run and see how it decreases your productivity and run time. This is sin, and it weighs a ton.

My stubborn will had failed. I had landed on the bottom of the ocean floor, my rock bottom. In my vision, in hindsight, I saw myself lying lifeless on the ocean floor. I had a real-life moment where I was lying on my bathroom floor. I had exasperated myself and lie there crying gut-wrenching sobs. I had given so much of myself and had received heartache in return. I'd compromised my dream of the white dress even though parts of that dream needed revision. At this point, the dress was shredded, pieces of cloth flapping through the water as I lay there—tears in more than one seam and tears in my soul like a bear's claw mark.

I was lying there motionless, without breath, and that breathlessness played out in reality too. During all of this toxicity it was hard to find air, anxiety struck. I couldn't catch my breath. There was a trip to the emergency room in the middle of the night—my mom and dad not fully knowing all I had let into my life, probably wondering how this anxiety crept its way in, but they were there with me. Anxiety was a reality that lasted almost a year. It set a lot of things back in my life. Not being able to catch your breath tempts your already frantic mind to panic more, and it is a very real, very scary thing.

Yet scary as it was, I'm thankful for it. God was going to use this to get my attention. I was finally afraid enough, desperate enough to seek Him. When finally a song lyric—I heard it somewhere deep within me—spoke to my heart: *"Open the eyes of my heart, Lord. I want to see you."*

I kept hearing this song. It was a song my mom would sing periodically when I was young. I was turning the key to my apartment in Brea, California, where I was living during that time, and that was the word I heard: "Lord." I hadn't ever called Jesus "Lord" before. But in a matter of a few weeks, I was experiencing Jesus and His love, and it was my new reality. It was as if He had been waiting for me to call His name, and as I did, a hand—Jesus's hand—reached down through the murky, churning waters, all the way down, down, down to the bottom of the ocean floor, and His hand picked up my form and lifted me out of that pit of despair. "Pull me from the trap my enemies set for me, for I find protection in you alone" (Ps. 31:4, NLT).

His hand lifted me out of the clutches of the deep, the place that had become a barren wilderness. He gently laid me back on a shore, an unknown shore. A brilliant, bright light was shining in my eyes as I opened them. I saw His face. I saw His gentle yet fiery eyes. He reached out His hand, inviting me to stand. It felt as if on wobbly knees, but I stood. My full weight was being put on Him. I couldn't stand on my own. I was weak. The best part? He didn't care what I looked like. I wasn't self-conscious about how I looked around Him. He looked at me past that and with a look of love, which was great because here I was emerged from the wreckage of my life, makeup streaked, dress ruined, yet I had someone to lean on: the Beloved, Christ, as I came out from the sea wilderness that my life had become. I turn to Matthew Henry, who illustrates the wilderness. He writes it as, "Wilderness, a sinful state…a wilderness, remote from communion with God, barren and dry, and in which there is no true comfort; it is a wandering wanting state. Out of this wilderness we are concerned to come up, by true repentance, in the strength of the grace of Christ, supported by our beloved and carried in his arms."[4]

Wandering and wanting, exactly the place I had been, a place of repentance was where I finally was.

I See You Dressed in White

I felt awake from my slumber, I was feeling delivered from my anxious thoughts, and as I began stumbling along the shore, walking inland and further from the churning waters, I saw a dense forest.

---

[4] I have learned so much from utilizing commentaries and writing down questions as I read the Bible. One of the most helpful tools I've discovered is Bible Study Tools online (www.biblestudytools.com) with one of my favorite google-searches being whatever Scripture I'm wanting to know more about and adding "Matthew Henry commentary" on the end of the search. I would need hours to sit and go through all of his lofty thoughts and when I've had the time I've done it. It's amazing how God's Spirit illuminates the pages of Scripture, these ancient texts and how they can be applied to our life today.

We had a journey to go on, we had to get going, and while I was still frail, I was not beyond repair. He knew everything because He'd been through it with me. I remembered the tear drop that fell and a few other handful of little moments like that. I was feeling overwhelmingly grateful for His strength, and His strength and power weren't used against me, it was a comfort. He was safe.

We made it to the forest's edge and came to a clearing. What I saw next in my vision was a large, looming white cross standing in a wide open field; the sun was setting. The golden light was creating a golden glow on the tips of the dry grass—almost as if the field were on fire. My heart surely was. There was something causing warmth within me like I'd never felt before. I made my way toward the cross. I bent low before it, and tears spilled as I realized for the first time what His love for me cost Him…His blood.

Pause for a little Bible lesson because this is important. I know we don't like to think about death, but it's something every person will face. For far too long I felt invincible, as if nothing could touch me. But again, that was so far from reality. I thought I could deal with my sin and mess later, but what if I never had that chance? What if my life was taken suddenly one of those drunken nights? By the grace of God that didn't happen. But not one of us is promised tomorrow. The law of sowing and reaping and sinning against a holy God meant the death penalty for me and eternal separation from God. "For the wages of sin is death but the free gift of God is eternal life in Christ Jesus our Lord" (Rom. 6:23, NIV).

It's like this…when we commit a crime, we break the law. When we sin, we break God's law. On earth, we might go to jail and have to go to court. Court can be a horrible place, especially when you're guilty. When I die, I am going to face God in a Heavenly Court of Law. What would I say when He finds me guilty of the charges stacked against me? All the lying, idolatry, impurities lurking in my heart never made right with Him? I'd have nothing to say. But in Christ, this won't be the case. We'll be welcomed in with loving arms, cleared of all debt. He's my defense attorney, and I will be able to walk through guilt free because He took the punishment for me. In our minds, we think if we're not a murderer or committing the "big sins," then why would we be sent to hell? The thing is this: God does not measure sin the way we do (Jm. 2:10) so that's what Romans 3:23 means when it says we have all sinned and fallen short of the glory of God. Every single one of us. Murderer or not, we're all guilty. And I cannot enter Heaven on my own merit. I'm not that powerful. I cannot clear my name of my sin. That's where Jesus comes in. "For God so loved the world, that he gave his only Son, that whoever believes in him shall not perish but have eternal life" (Jn. 3:16, NIV). And in that verse is the gospel.

"**G**od's **O**nly **S**on **P**erished **E**ternal **L**ife." And that's the good news, the **GOSPEL**! You're standing on death row spiritually, you've been found guilty on all sin counts, and Jesus—your advocate, the best defense attorney, the Judge—stepped down off the bench and said, "I'm going to go die for you." Who would do that? Who could do that? Nobody but Him.

Jesus died. In *my* place—and in *your* place—so that we may live eternally and have the forgiveness of sin and escape death. *This* is love—self-sacrificing, "giving up His life for us" love. This is the ultimate demonstration of it. Because who but Jesus has died for you? A sinless, perfect man demonstrating His perfect love dying for a sin-filled, guilty as heck humanity. Again, no one but Him.

Okay, now back to my vision: Condemning thoughts from the enemy filled my mind at the foot of that cross in that field. How could one so vile, so full of sin be worthy to stand before such holiness and think I could have that pretty white dress restored? But in my vision as I was kneeling before the cross, I saw Jesus approach me, and He knelt beside me. Not drawing me up but coming down to meet me right where I was. Feeling as if I couldn't even lift my eyes to meet His gaze, I felt Him lift my chin to look into His eyes, and He wiped my tears. As I met His gaze, my hard heart began to soften. I was able to receive His love, and I felt His love opening up my heart—answering those words that were sung in the depth of my battered soul, *"Open the eyes of my heart."* I realized I *wasn't* worthy, but Jesus is. He is the worthy Lamb who was slain, and in Him, I am worthy and was no longer lost but finally found. "How much more, then, will the blood of Christ, who through the eternal Spirit offered himself unblemished to God, cleanse our consciences from acts that lead to death, so that we may serve the living God!" (Heb. 9:14, NIV).

A new identity was given to me there, an identity based on Scripture, which held these truths. I was:

> [a] No longer a slave, but free.
> [b] A part of the body of Christ, a part of a family.
> [c] Royal.
> [d] Redeemed, bought with a price; Valuable.
> [e] A child of God, daughter of the King.

Here are the matching Scripture references for you to hold so that you can claim your identity when the devil wants to make you feel diminished or devalued.

> [a] "We know that our old sinful selves were crucified with Christ so that sin might lose its power in our lives. We are no longer slaves to sin" (Rom. 6:6, NLT).

[b] "Now you are the body of Christ, and each one of you is a part of it" (1 Cor. 12:27, NIV).

[c] "But you are a chosen people, a royal priesthood, a holy nation, God's special possession, that you may declare the praises of him who called you out of darkness into his wonderful light" (1 Pet. 2:9, NIV).

[d] "Do you not know that your bodies are temples of the Holy Spirit, who is in you, whom you have received from God? You are not your own; you were bought at a price. Therefore honor God with your bodies" (1 Cor. 6:19–20, NIV).

[e] "Yet to all who did receive him, to those who believed in his name, he gave the right to become children of God" (Jn. 1:12, NIV).

In one moment, I became valuable, treasured, and was an heiress. I looked down to see my stained, ripped dress was solid white. "And all who have been united with Christ in baptism have put on Christ, like putting on new clothes" (Gal. 3:27, NLT). He had forgiven all my past, present, and future sin and would toss any trace of it out into the ocean, never to think about the past or bring those things up ever again. "Once again you will have compassion on us. You will trample our sins under your feet and throw them into the depths of the ocean!" (Mic. 7:19, NIV). The place I had felt I'd once been—the ocean floor—is where my sins had gone, never to be used against me or brought up again. His words were used to build me up, not beat me down. I could believe once more in the white dress and believe one day I might wear one. And this is where redemption happened. I would see Him retrace parts of my past and watch

Him write over the bad parts with stories filled with hope, joy, and restored peace. These stories, along with the white dress, would be used to tell of His glory.

"Don't copy the behavior and customs of this world, but let God transform you into a new person by changing the way you think. Then you will learn to know God's will for you, which is good and pleasing and perfect."

— Romans 12:2

3

The Veil

"But whenever anyone turns to the Lord, the veil is taken away.
Now the Lord is the Spirit, and where the
Spirit of the Lord is, there is freedom.
And we all, who with unveiled faces contemplate the Lord's glory,
are being transformed into his image with ever-increasing glory,
which comes from the Lord, who is the Spirit."
— 2 Corinthians 3:16–18

I now knew where that innate desire for perfection came from. My heart was longing for the only perfect Man, Jesus. And I got to be with Him! Every second of every day. He chose me long before I chose Him (Eph. 1:4; 1 Jn. 4:19). On this journey, I was relieved to know that my heart and future were safe and secure in being in a relationship with Jesus. Nothing else mattered like it once did. I stood on the truth that I now belonged to Jesus Christ and that I'd been saved from sin and death because of His death and resurrection. And the relationships I once pursued paled in comparison to His extravagant love for me. He showed me as a woman, I need not pursue any man. In God's perfect timing, He would lead that right man to pursue me. He'd speak a word to his heart.

Nonetheless, there would be a very long, very tedious road ahead.

The Path to Purity

Some of the stops along this road would be purity and patience—especially for this redeemed dream of one day being married. There was a lot of heart work to be done first. My heart had a lot of built-up residue. A heart that's tolerated years of abuse doesn't heal overnight. I believed that I had been forgiven, but there was also a lot of purging to go through. At the foot of the cross I found forgiveness for my sin, yet I'd have to continue to go there to remind myself of this forgiveness, and learning what it meant to live out the gospel daily would be a continual, daily occurrence. There were moments of stumbling along the path, where my feet tripped up, but God swiftly grabbed my elbow before I hit the ground and helped me stand back up. "*Keep going,*" He would say kindly to my heart.

I've found there's another sort of wilderness, and I felt that's exactly where Jesus and I were. This wilderness was "an empty, pathless area or region." It's where I would learn to trust Him when the path seemed uncertain. I'd also be learning what it meant to daily die to myself and what living in purity meant. That sinful, willful state wanted to keep rearing its ugly head and tempt me to go back the way I came—to live for self and ditch any sort of life dependent on God. But life with Jesus was too sweet, that fire within kept burning and the truth of Galatians 2:20 was the place I lived my life from now. "I have been crucified with Christ and I no longer live, but Christ lives in me. The life I now live in the body, I live by faith in the Son of God, who loved me and gave himself for me."

"Then Jesus said to his disciples, "If any of you wants to be my follower, you must give up your own way, take up your cross, and follow me" (Matt. 16:24, NLT). As we kept walking, I was called off the path of sameness and comfort, but weirdly enough, I had so much peace. Even though I didn't know where we were going or what was ahead, knowing you're in God's will for your life brings peace of mind. I had nothing left to hide. Nothing to cover up. It was all laid down at the foot of the cross. He knew everything about me and still loved me, and that was refreshing. I also knew the Lord calling me out of my comfort zone had purpose, and it was to cause growth and maturity in me. If I'd known then just what that meant, that He'd call me to tasks I'd never dreamed I was capable of accomplishing, or had ever dreamt for myself, I probably wouldn't have believed it, one of those being a small business owner.

Tearing of the Veil

As a wedding photographer, I've witnessed many weddings, and one of the most significant parts of the wedding ceremony is when the bride walks down the aisle toward her groom. If she chooses to go the traditional route, she will have a veil covering her face that her groom will lift when she reaches him at the end of the aisle, revealing his bride. The Bible talks about a very significant tearing of *the* veil, which symbolized granting us access to a holy God.

Something happened in the Temple at the very moment that Christ died on the cross. Mark 15:37–38 tells us when He died, "Jesus uttered a loud cry, and breathed His last. And the veil of the temple was torn in two from top to bottom" (see also Matthew 27:51). Luke's eyewitness account says, "The light from the sun was gone. And suddenly, the curtain in the sanctuary of the Temple was torn down the middle" (Lk. 23:45, NLT). The veil is symbolic of the incarnate life of Jesus, and the tearing of the veil was His death on the cross. The death of Christ opened a new way into the presence of God. "Sure, the Veil was beautiful, but it was not the beautiful Veil that made entrance into God's presence possible. The only way a guilty sinner could pass to the other side of the Veil into the

Holy of Holies and live was by way of the sprinkling of the blood of the sacrifice. It was by the blood of atonement that the way into the throne room of God was opened. There is only one way into God's holy presence; it is the blood of sacrifice."[5] Before Jesus atoned for our sins, the Old Testament goes into great detail of how specifically sin had to be dealt with, and it included the spilling of animal blood. I was learning that is why Jesus was called "the Lamb of God," He was the final and ultimate sin sacrifice.

For me, repentance did—and didn't—just happen overnight. There was a building up to a moment where I finally felt like the veil was torn from my eyes, helping me to see. This moment was very memorable because I was confronted with a situation that I was very accustomed to, but suddenly I was uncomfortable and suddenly saw sin for what it was (unholy) and God for who He truly is (holy). This unveiling happened about a couple of years after my panic attacks, a few months after the bathroom floor, and right before I knew I wanted to give my whole life to Jesus. If we rewind to the bathroom floor scene, once I gained composure, I plopped down on my bed and picked up a devotional book called *Daily Light Devotional* by Anne Graham Lotz that my mom had given me. The devotional is a compilation of Scripture morning and night to make one cohesive message for both times of the day. The words on the page spoke deeply into the hurting places of my heart. The Scripture for that particular date spoke so specifically to what I was going through I felt seen to the depths of my innermost thoughts. Was God really that near?

I tested it each day. Every time the words for that day from Scripture jumped off the page into my heart. Whether I knew it or not, morning and night I was being cleansed by the washing of the Word of God, which is holy and true, and it was dismantling all

---

[5] Cited from Wil Pounds, *Abide in Christ*, online.

the unholy and untrue things I'd allowed in. I began falling asleep praying silent prayers to God, and I began to see Him answer them. Before any of this was happening in my life, I had purchased tickets to a music festival with a group of friends. I wasn't sure I still wanted to go or if I should go, but my heart still had plans and motives for wanting to go, having an excuse to get all dressed up (three different outfits for three different days) and knowing I was dressing to impress. Feeling good by looking good gives you a false sense of power for a moment, because you affect the way a person acts, thinks, and behaves, and you feel in control. It's also a great boost to the ego. It's what I was used to doing.

But one thing was different now, after being saturated in Scripture from the devotional, I was more aware of how I did and did not want to act. I made a decision in my heart to "put a guard over my lips" (Ps. 141:3), which was one of the Scriptures I read from the devotional for that weekend's dates. To me that meant being cautious as to what I was consuming and not thoughtlessly drinking the weekend away.

I slipped. I did have a few drinks, but I remember the alcohol having very little to almost no effect on me. As I consumed it, I wanted it out of my system. It felt foreign to me, which was new. I had this really cool thought of how God's Word is referred to as the "bread of life." In the same way that eating bread will soak up or slow down the absorption rate of alcohol, and because I had so much of the Word in me, it was causing my body to slow down the absorption rate of the alcohol. The Holy Spirit comes to live inside of you when you receive Christ. He is the Word (Jn. 1:1-5).

The moment that changed everything for me, the unveiling, was the second night of this three-day weekend. The later the night gets, the more intoxicated everyone gets, and it was getting pretty late. I followed the pack into a tent with a stage, a tent called the Sahara Tent. This tent was the one with the electric dance music, not really my cup of tea to begin with. People were raging to the noise, and there was hardly any space to even walk in. It was a sweaty, blurred mess. The speakers and lights are what I remember most. The lights were obnoxious, the sound deafening. In that instant, all I could see before me was depravity. I hadn't ever used that word before in my life, but here I was feeling like that's what this was. Almost as if in slow motion, I saw people cackling, blitzed out, rolling on drugs. What didn't sit well with me was the way people were lifting their hands, closing their eyes, in worship. It was the worship of the music, the DJ who was elevated high above the crowd, and a worship of feelings, people completely given over to their carnal pleasures. I heard His Voice above the noise—inside my soul, the same voice that sang the lyrics of the song my mom used to sing. *"You're going to need to make a choice right now. You can't have Me and have this too."*

Honestly, there's never been an easier choice. I was done. Once and for all. No more half-hearted following. I wanted all in and to set out steadfastly on this journey with Jesus, who met me at the cross, who saved me from myself, and who set me gently on the shore. I pushed my way through the sea of people and didn't look back. I walked in with a group of people, but I walked out alone. Well, not really alone, hand in hand with my Savior. As I walked out of that tent, I said to God, "I'm Yours." I meant that with my whole heart.

Soul Ties

As you can tell, the coming out of living life dictated by the flesh and learning what it means to live by the Spirit is a trial-and-error and error covered by grace type of journey. I mentioned stumbling in the clearing as I "Bambi-leg" walked with Jesus for the first time. I still had people and things in my life that needed to be cut out, which was a process that contributed to some of the trip ups. One of the trip ups being falling back into sin with someone even though I was becoming more aware of God's presence now in my life.

God knows our frailties, He knows our weaknesses. God allowed me to make these mistakes because through them I would learn His mercy and grace, how much I needed Him, to hear His voice more clearly, and He wanted to test my faith. By His grace I didn't let those trip ups cause me to give up. I didn't just throw in the towel and say, "I messed up, I might as well go back to my old ways; that was a nice try." No, it made me more determined to cling all the more tightly to Him because I knew I did not want to live as a slave to that lifestyle anymore. I had to learn to be honest with myself. Did I really need to go to *that* place where that person would be to "shine light"? That was my excuse at first, "I'll just go to that bar and shine my light for Jesus."

It's really all I knew, and in His lovingkindness, He actually even did that. He used me to minister in the only places I had known for so long, bars. After the music festival, He miraculously took any desire for alcohol away. I was able to talk about my newfound faith with old friends. I would tell my friends "no, thank you" to the shot or vodka cranberry not because I was a "good Christian" now but because I genuinely did not want it. One friend even told me he used to have a Bible and hadn't read it in years but said he was going to try and find it. People asked what was happening in my life because I went from being the "taking three shots in one night" type to sipping on water, and I got to testify that this was Christ in me. But there eventually came a time I had to step away and do other things. Note to the young woman, friend, reader who has made it this far in the story, He doesn't want His daughters in dingy, dark places. He has so many more quality options than those and so many different and new places He wants to take you.

The one particular trip up had a lot to do with not knowing about purity and not knowing the power of a soul tie. After that night, I vowed wholeheartedly to stay pure and wait on the Lord to bring me a God-fearing man and asked Him to help me reserve my heart for him. But more than that, it caused me to see how serious I was in my love for Jesus and that I didn't want anything to come between me and Him.

Part of the journey in your relationship with God begins with trusting that He knows best. It will require giving up some of the things you've allowed your heart to attach to. It may even be that two-year-long relationship you've invested a lot of your time and heart into, but I promise, letting God take over in that part of your life is something you will never regret. We are at the part in my journey that He began the painstaking process of taking away some of the things I'd known for so long, things that were familiar, and I found myself having to relinquish control. I was actually sometimes in physical pain as the pruning began.

I felt the sting of the tears as I allowed Him to remove people from my life who were causing more harm than good. It was painful because I had let my heart attach to something God never intended it to attach to. This detachment was something I could have avoided had I let Him into my heart sooner. Yet God in His mercy cared that I still cared for them; He cared for them even more. He gave me plenty of opportunities to share my new faith in Christ and point them to this newfound love for my Savior and share the message of Christ and the cross that saved me. Everyone's response was different, some denied the power of the gospel at work in my life, some were affected and listened intently.

Regardless of whether they believed me or not, or whether they were ready to receive Christ into their hearts or not, I could still pray for them. This is a verse that spoke encouragement when I was feeling discouraged when some of the people I loved weren't understanding. "We use God's mighty weapons, not worldly weapons, to knock down the strongholds of human reasoning and to destroy false arguments. We destroy every proud obstacle that keeps people from knowing God. We capture their rebellious thoughts and teach them to obey Christ" (2 Cor. 10:4–5, NLT). That would be the spiritual weapon to tear down strongholds in others' lives. Speaking of the spiritual, here's that thing I keep mentioning: soul ties. There are some things we will carry into our marriages, "baggage" some might call it. It matters what we choose to attach our hearts to in our years of singleness. Thankfully, God's grace covers us, and He does restore much of what was lost or wasted during those years if purity was lost. He can give it back. But I say this next part to really emphasize the part of marriage that gets robbed because another lie our culture sells us is that sex outside of marriage is normal, thrilling, and glamorized, and sex inside marriage is boring and monotonous.

Sex should also be treated the same way marriage should be viewed, sacred. Our souls become tied or bound to people we are vulnerable with, and what is more vulnerable than being that intimate with someone? The security that comes with sex in the boundaries of marriage is how it was always intended by God. He created sex, and He created it to be enjoyed between a husband and a wife, and it has a purpose. Sex without commitment leaves you hurt and leaves you exposed. When we're intimate with someone who isn't our spouse, telling them we love them binds us to them. Telling someone, "I love you" in a romantic way is powerful. An attachment happens. There is life and death in the power of the tongue, "The tongue can bring death or life; those who love to talk will reap the consequences (Prov. 18:21, NLT). What we speak to one another matters, and when you bring in the physical element of sex, even more attachment grows.

There are reasons God reserves sex and intimacy of relationships for marriage. Read what Mark 10:6–9 has to say about sex and intimacy, "But from the beginning of creation, 'God made them male and female.' 'Therefore a man shall leave his father and mother and hold fast to his wife, and the two shall become one flesh.' So they are no longer two but one flesh. What therefore God has joined together, let not man separate."

You are not meant to separate after joining together. But that's what happens. It is literally the opposite of self-sacrificing, what Jesus models and how He loves, it's serving self. Not that sex within marriage won't have its qualms to work out. We are still dealing with two sinners, but there is a bond, a sacredness when there is a commitment made to one another, which is partly the sacrificing of self.

I once had the privilege of sharing my testimony at a purity conference with middle school– and high school–aged girls. One of the word pictures/demonstrations from one of the speakers that day stuck with me. The speaker invited a girl and a boy to stand up on stage, and she handed them both pieces of duct tape. She directed them to come together and put the two pieces of tape together. Once the two pieces of tape had stuck together, she asked them to do their best to pull them apart. As you can guess, or even try for yourself, it was nearly impossible to remove one piece of tape from the other. What pieces they did pull apart were little broken bits of tape. It was such an accurate portrait of what we are doing each time we give our bodies to another person outside of marriage, more and more is taken from us as you attempt to separate—and sadly, more and more is taken from our future spouse.

So the question to ask yourself is, "What are you binding yourself to? Is it a good thing or a God thing?" Read this, "A soul tie is like a linkage in the soul realm between two people. It links their souls together, which can bring forth beneficial results or negative results. The negative effect of a soul tie: soul ties can also be used for the devil's advantage. Soul ties formed from sex outside of marriage cause a person to become defiled. In a godly marriage, God links the two together and the Bible tells us that they become one flesh. As a result of them becoming one flesh, it binds them together and they will cleave onto one another in a unique way. The purpose of this cleaving is to build a very healthy, strong and close relationship between a man and a woman."[6]

This gives us a clear definition of what a soul tie is and how powerful the bond created through oneness is. To save yourself for marriage is something that will take great conviction, determination, and accountability.

Pura Vida

That next year, 2014, was a whirlwind of a year between serving on a mission field in Haiti and the Philippines. Right in between both of those two really big trips the Lord allowed me to take a trip to Costa Rica. It felt like a honeymoon after enduring some really hard things in Haiti. He gave me this trip, and everywhere I turned I saw the words "Pura Vida." I even bought a wood carved sign that said these words, and it's in my room as a reminder and a mark of what God did in my heart there. The fight for purity and to wait to have sex until marriage is hard and is not popular and rarely celebrated. You might even face ridicule or awkward avoidances of the

---

[6] This book, *Passion and Purity* by Elisabeth Elliott, helped me view passion and purity like I never had before.

subject altogether, but as a new creation in Christ, if you've dedicated your life to Him, do not resist this part. It's a good thing. You're letting God's love grow where the world's weeds were taking over.

If you have ever experienced growing pains, you can relate to the pain they cause. I remember I'd lie in bed at night when I was young, feeling so much pain in my legs, feeling so restless. I even writhed through the pain some nights, it was that excruciating. But I survived. And it was all for the sake of growing healthy, strong, and tall. It was a momentary pain that I now am passed. In the same way, I look at what God requires. The extraction of things is painful, but it is to bring about the most growth much like growing pains. Making new decisions in my life like I never had before was going to make me restless at times, but it would be worth it.

I was now inviting Him in and asking Him for guidance about everything. I knew He knew that I wanted to choose Him over anything. I know He saw my heart, and it was set on pleasing Him. New thoughts lived where impure thoughts once lived (Rom. 12:2). He was patient with me while I figured it out. There were some things I'd done that couldn't ever be undone. Sometimes we have to live with the consequences of our actions, and sometimes it just takes time to heal the wounds. One of those consequences was a tattoo I had chosen to put on my body. The words read, "There once was a little girl who never knew love until he broke her heart." Yep. That is a tattoo I have on my body. Without going into the full account of how and why this is now permanently on my body, it's very telling of where my heart was when I got it. It was breaking or rather had been broken. I don't think about the tattoo often, and it's in a place where I don't have to look at it daily. God has given me new perspective on it and shows how He can redeem anything. I once meditated on the words to gain more insight into this broken girl I once knew so well. The Lord emphasized or prompted me to stay a little longer on the word "broke." With that word in the forefront of my mind, God used a quote from Elisabeth Elliot's *Passion and Purity* once again. I was reading it around the same time this quiet reflection was happening. She writes, "One morning I was reading the story of Jesus' feeding of the five thousand. The disciples could only find five loaves of bread and two fishes. 'Let me have them,' said Jesus. He asked for all. He took them, said the blessing, and *broke* them before He gave them out. I remembered what a chapel speaker, Ruth Stull of Peru, had said, 'If my life is broken when given to Jesus, it is because pieces will feed a multitude, while a loaf will satisfy only a little lad.'"

There was a reassurance to me as I read those words. No matter the "he" who attempted to break me, it was the "He" that could use these broken pieces of my story that could feed a multitude. Jesus had a purpose for my broken heart. And you might think your heart can only break so many times. This wasn't the last time my heart would break. It would continue to be beautifully broken for things God's heart breaks for too.

"But then I will win her back once again.
I will lead her into the desert and speak tenderly to her there.
I will return her vineyards to her
and transform the Valley of Trouble into a gateway of hope.
She will give herself to me there, as she did long ago when
she was young,
when I freed her from her captivity in Egypt."

— Hosea 2:14–15

4

Lasting Beauty and The Vow

"I will make you my wife forever, showing you
righteousness and justice,
unfailing love and compassion. I will be faithful to you
and make you mine
and you will finally know me as the LORD"
— Hosea 3:19–20

R egardless of a messy past and continual rejection of His love,
He will take drastic measures to win us back to Himself, to
woo us and romance us. He romances us through His Word. Words
such as, "It was your right hand and strong arm and the *blinding
light from your face* that helped them, for you loved them" (Ps. 44:3,
emphasis mine), as a literal streak of bright light reflected off the
neighbor's sun reflector onto my face. More tears flowed. How
could they not?

These weren't coincidences. These are what I call "God-
incidences" that were happening every day. Reassurances of His
presence and His seeing me. Everything I was experiencing of God
through His Word was speaking life and healing and comfort into
my weariness. There was a peace that surpassed all understanding
like Scripture promised (Phil. 4:7). The freedom I found in Christ
was what unbound me from my impulsive tendencies, and this

wasn't me trying to be better for the sake of "being Christian," it was the Holy Spirit purifying me and helping me with self-control, and for the first time my actions met my words. Like I said, I was able to turn down the alcohol offered to me. I had always said after a long weekend of drinking that "I was so done drinking," but I always wound up drinking the very next weekend. Now, I was filled with and empowered by the Spirit at work within me and had no room for the spirits. I was being positioned for a transition that was about to happen. In the fall of that 2013 year, I signed up for Bible study at the church I had grown up going to.

For the first time ever, there was no place I'd rather be than at church. That's when you know it's real. No one had to tell me to go, force me out of bed to go, like my mom had to when I was in high school. I just knew I wanted to be in the presence of God and His people. What better place than back to my roots and what better way to begin than by doing an in-depth study of the Word of God, which my church offered.

I was in my last semester at Cal State Long Beach getting my bachelor's degree in fashion merchandising (which is why I went to Paris—it was a very surreal, fashion-filled school trip). This determination to go deeper in the Word took this unsure, still timid girl to the first day of Bible study alone. That was going to be a common theme for quite some time—doing things out of my comfort zone and not being afraid to try something or go somewhere without knowing anyone. I sat in one of the last rows that first night of Bible study. I was more comfortable observing from the back and taking it all in from there. I couldn't become fully immersed in the worship portion of the night because if I closed my eyes, I wouldn't be able to read the words on the screen, I knew none of them by heart. I hadn't heard worship songs in such a long time, and these ones were new to me.

What was introduced that night was the study titled *Simply Jesus.* We would be going through the Old and New Testaments and would be tracing the scarlet thread of Jesus's love through the entire Bible. That was news to me, that Jesus could be found in the Old Testament. I knew the accounts of His life and ministry were in the gospels of Matthew, Mark, Luke, and John, but it would be interesting to find out how we could find Him in books in the Old Testament, books such as Isaiah, 1 Samuel, Ruth, Genesis, Hosea, and others.

I consider myself an "Old Testament" girl now. You know those chapters that list out king's names, tribes and nations, rules and regulations that can feel like a long history lesson? Well, God even opened my eyes to read those chapters in a new light, and I couldn't get enough. The Bible was coming alive, and I was excited to apply its truths to my life. I was learning more than I expected and writing every question I had down in my journal. When you look for Jesus throughout *all* the Scriptures with an open heart, you will most definitely find Him. "Search the book of the LORD, and see what He will do" (Isa. 34:16, NLT).

I've enjoyed reading Scripture alongside commentaries to help me better understand what I'm reading or to answer some of my pending questions. One of those helpful commentaries comes from Matthew Henry, an author from the Reformation period, aka the 1500s, and he eloquently explains what it means to seek the Scriptures: "It is spoken to us in the nature of an advice, or a command to all Christians to search the scriptures. All those who would find Christ must search the scriptures; not only read them, and hear them, but search them. Diligence in seeking, labor, and study and close application of mind and the desire and design of finding. We must aim at some spiritual benefit and advantage in reading and studying the scripture, and often ask, 'What am I now searching for?' We must search as for hidden treasures (Prov. 2:4), as those that sink for gold or silver, or that dive for pearl (Job. 28:1–11)."

Every part of the Bible is ultimately to know more about the character of God and who He is even though it also speaks into our lives as we seek its pages for answers to life's biggest questions. All of my life, when I read the Bible, I was only asking, "How does this story apply to me?" Yet I was learning there was wisdom in not just looking for it to speak to me about me but to teach me more about the things of God. When we came to the week of studying the Book of Hosea in Bible study, I positioned myself for application. Surprisingly, the story of the prophet Hosea was about to speak into my life as well as showing me more of who God is to me, His role in my life, and who I'd been to Him.

The Unfaithful Wife

I was reading the brief introduction to Hosea, and I automatically began reading as if I were in the prophet Hosea's place. Hosea—a prophet called by God to marry a prostitute and to love her despite her infidelity. Okay, I could relate to that having known what it felt like to be cheated on in a relationship. I tapped into those feelings so I could understand more of what Hosea must have been feeling. However, as the chapters went on, I realized Hosea was a portrait of God and His enduring love for a sin-filled humanity. This was another story about Israel's unfaithfulness and continual rejection and turning back to idols after God had repeatedly taken them back and held back His wrath showing Himself faithful and merciful to a faithless and rebellious people.

I was still thinking I was the Hosea of the story (which meant I was putting myself in the place of God) because I could identify with him from an earthly standpoint, comparing old relationships to that. Wasn't I the one who remained faithful, while all those guys had been unfaithful? "I sure had!" was my indignant response. Little did I know I was utterly unaware, my perspective askew, and I was about to be corrected and called out to who I really was in this story. Because it didn't matter so much about those earthly relationships that didn't serve me, but it mattered about my relationship with God, whom I was being called to serve.

Another pause for a brief synopsis on this book of the Bible. God called the prophet Hosea to marry a woman, Gomer, who was a prostitute. Gomer continued to go back to her lovers and fine living even after Hosea married her, which was symbolic of God pursuing His chosen people, the Israelites, relentlessly, fearlessly, and demonstrating covenant love toward them despite their rejection.

God's redeeming love, faithfulness, and stern warnings toward the nation of Israel is the main theme of all the books of the Bible in the Old Testament. It documents Israel's history, and it's important to know that God is the Hebrew God of Israel, and it's the country that redemption would come out of, it is the country of Jesus's lineage. In the book of Hosea, God uses the portrait of marriage as an example of His covenant relationship with His people. Referencing back to Christ's love for the Church, in Ephesians 5, and the command for husbands to love their wives in this same "lay down your life" type of love, wives are commanded to demonstrate their commitment through submission to their husbands. Their role is equally a portrait of Christ as He submitted to the Father's will of dying a sinner's death on a cross to redeem the world. In summation, a husband and wife's role is to build a reciprocal relationship based on love and respect, which is a demonstration of what God desired from His covenant, chosen people.

You might be wondering what I'm even talking about. One of the couples I've interviewed for The Marriage Project did a beautiful job in describing covenant, submission, and our role as the Church and Israel's role in God's plan. Vanessa Vanzyl shared in episode 10 of The Marriage Project, "In our gender roles, God has asked us to submit, but it doesn't mean you have to be quiet. As wives, we are life givers. In Hebrew, it's the word 'ezer,' and the only other place the word 'ezer' is used is for the Holy Spirit. We literally get to be this inner life-giving presence for our husbands. It's such a strong, powerful word, a military word. We get to submit everything—our ideas and opinions—to them, but ultimately God asks us to trust Him and our husband enough to make the final call. God knew there'd be a battle if that wasn't clearly defined."

Her husband, Rehgert Vanzyl, includes this to husbands, "This isn't permission to oppress. If we as husbands submit to God, then my wife will want to submit and serve and be a part of this team." Now as for covenant, in a broken world full of broken promises it can be hard to fathom an idea like covenant. Covenant is an everlasting promise to be faithful and to love indefinitely. As in Hosea and many other places in Scripture, God made countless promises to Israel, and He's made a new Covenant through Christ with His Church. God's design for marriage was to reflect His Covenant and commitment with His chosen people. The whole Bible is a marriage covenant. It's about the Bridegroom pursuing His bride, God pursuing His people.

There are countless examples of God's chosen people, the Israelites, promising to remain true to Him throughout Scripture, but we see that not too long after their commitment, whether a generation or two pass, they are right back to worshipping other gods and manmade idols (one such example is in Judges 1–3). They were more interested in gratifying themselves rather than making or keeping a commitment they had made to God. Sounded familiar. So many questions went through my mind as I finished reading the first three chapters of Hosea. "Why would God ask Hosea to marry a woman He knew would be unfaithful to him?" As I asked, God began to answer, and I was beginning to understand. Verses from Hosea would be the next marker in my walk with Jesus, and with a mention of Egypt in Hosea 2:15, I laughed because it was in Egypt where "she (*Israel)*" was freed from captivity. I, too, began to taste freedom in the Sahara Tent, and last time I checked part of the Sahara Desert is in Egypt—the irony was not lost on me.

The piercing words found in Hosea chapter 2 helped me see my sin from God's vantage point and see it as severely as they were stated here. There is no sugar-coating these verses in the Book of Hosea. We might think we can sugar-coat or cover up any part of our life, especially our sin. We might fool ourselves and other people, but there's no fooling Jesus. He sees every part of our heart and still pursues us.

There are a lot of methods He uses to expose the truth of the state of our heart, His Word being number one, but don't reject that friend trying to speak the truth to you in love; God uses them too. Read here, "To learn, you must love discipline; it is stupid to hate correction" (Prov. 12:1, NLT); "For the word of God is alive and powerful. It is sharper than the sharpest two-edged sword, cutting between soul and spirit, between joint and marrow. It exposes our innermost thoughts and desires" (Heb. 4:12, NLT).

The words in Hosea did their job of piercing through, yet surprisingly they began to bind me up at the same time. Reading the first half of Hosea chapter 2 was like reading a page from the biography of my life in those years of living in sin. I had seen sin for what it was in the desert and found forgiveness at the cross, but had I really taken inventory of all my sin yet? The daily sin. I needed to realize this because it would cause me to admit I wasn't the victim of circumstances—or Hosea. I was Gomer. I had been the unfaithful wife to the Lord, and I had worshipped other gods over the Creator, breaking commandment numbers one and two.

I had caused the Lord's heart to break when I decided to chase after idols, giving myself over and over again to relationships. I just sat in that moment for a while and said through wet eyes, "I'm so sorry, God." After salvation, there is a lifelong process called sanctification, and the theme of sanctification seems to be a lot of crying. Tears of repentance. Tears of joy. Tears of thanksgiving. It's one thing to receive salvation and believe in Jesus, but it's a whole other thing to continually repent because we're prone to wander and leave our First Love, similar to Israel and their forgetting their Creator. I saw God's love in a different way for me here. Whereas at the cross, it was a gentle touch, this was a wooing type of love.

There was someone who fought for me, had chosen me, and adored me and remained faithful when I hadn't. I wondered more about who Gomer was and what her story could have possibly looked like. Did she worship approval and acceptance, and this was her way of receiving such validation—selling herself to men? What was she willing to put on and give out just to receive pretty things instead of receiving love from her husband?

I began trying to take the lens off me and search the Scripture to know more about who God is. Like I said, some of the first parts of Hosea 2 are hard to get through. Is God a cruel God? No. He's a man of His word. If He is the God of Hosea 2:14–23 (the redemptive parts), He has to be the God of Hosea 2:1–13 (the harder parts). He may slay us with thirst, but it's all to win us back. He may strip us bare, but He covers us (1 Pet. 4:8). He allows the desert, the barren wilderness place, so that we're so destitute we become dependent on Him once more or for the first time ever.

He had already begun to transform my valley of trouble into a gateway of hope. It was a beautiful thing. He *did* win me back to

Himself (Hosea 2:14) when He had nothing to prove. I had heard so many empty promises made from guys, promises that they'd change in an effort to win me back after they'd hurt me and cheated me. I fell for that too many times. They never changed and only hurt me more. And yet here I was, the unfaithful one to God, and He went out of *His* way to pursue me? Shouldn't it have been me trying to prove to Him I was worthy of His love? But that's not who God is. We have nothing to prove. He simply loves us, and He keeps the commitments He makes to us.

I want to type this Scripture out in full so you can read it too.

When the LORD first began speaking to Israel through Hosea, he said to him, "Go and marry a prostitute so some of her children will be born to you from other men. This will illustrate the way my people have been untrue to me, openly committing adultery against the LORD by worshiping other gods (Hosea 1:2).

But now, call Israel to account, for she is no longer my wife, and I am no longer her husband.

Tell her to take off her garish makeup and suggestive clothing and to stop playing the prostitute.

If she doesn't, I will strip her as naked as she was on the day she was born.

I will leave her to die of thirst, as in a desert or a dry and barren wilderness.

And I will not love her children as I would my own because they are not my children!

They were conceived in adultery.

For their mother is a shameless prostitute and became pregnant in a shameful way.

She said, "I'll run after other lovers and sell myself to them for food and drink, for clothing of wool and linen, and for olive oil."

But I will fence her in with thorn bushes.

I will block the road to make her lose her way.

When she runs after her lovers, she won't be able to catch up with them.

She will search for them but not find them.

Then she will think, "I might as well return to my husband because I was better off with him than I am now."

She doesn't realize that it was I who gave her everything she has—the grain, the wine, the olive oil. Even the gold and silver she used in worshiping the god Baal were gifts from me!

But now I will take back the wine and ripened grain, I generously provided each harvest season. I will take away the linen and wool clothing I gave her to cover her nakedness. I will strip her naked in public, while her other lovers look on. No one will be able to rescue her from my hands. I will put an end to her annual festivals, her new moon celebrations, and her Sabbath days—all her appointed festivals. I will destroy her vineyards and orchards, things she claims her lovers gave her.

I will let them grow into tangled thickets, where only wild animals will eat the fruit.

I will punish her for all the times she deserted me, when she burned incense to her images of Baal, put on her earrings and jewels, and went out looking for her lovers," says the LORD (Hos. 2:2–13, NLT).

But also:

But, I will win her back once again. I will lead her out into the desert and speak tenderly to her there. I will return her vineyards to her and transform the valley of trouble into a gateway of hope. She will give herself to me there as she did long ago when she was young, when I freed her from her captivity in Egypt. "In that coming day," says the LORD, "you will call me 'my husband' instead of 'my master.'"

O Israel, I will cause you to forget your images of Baal; even their names will no longer be spoken. At that time I will make a covenant with all the wild animals, and the birds and the animals that scurry along the grounds so that they will not harm you. I will remove all weapons of war from the land, all swords and bows, so you can live unafraid in peace and safety.

I will make you my wife forever, showing you righteousness and justice, unfailing love and compassion. I will be faithful to you and make you mine, and you will finally know me as LORD (Hos. 2:14–20, NLT).

This was tough love. This was what I needed to hear. I grew in my knowledge of Him through this week in Bible study. And I knew the difference with the stripping of the world vs. the stripping mentioned in verse two of Hosea. When you strip for the world, it leaves you shivering, feeling ashamed for baring all. God strips us down so He can clean us up. In the same way bed sheets are stripped to remove odors or oils, so He's stripping us of the residue of sin that remains. He doesn't leave us shivering. His Word drapes a quilt around our shivering shoulders and cleans up the exposed parts that feel like raw, open wounds.

I wonder if there was confusion for Gomer when a man entered her life and wanted to love her despite her flaws and her waywardness. I'd imagine she didn't know how to receive such extravagant love or distrusted it. Perhaps she felt she didn't have anything she could offer this man or maybe she thought what he wanted was external beauty, never having been taught the value of a beautiful heart, mind, and soul. Perhaps the world hadn't given her a chance to develop that; harsh and showy was the world's standard of beauty, and she'd owned it. Her lovers got the made-up version of herself, the version she thought they wanted. She probably thought that such showiness would turn Hosea away, but he persisted. He loved her gently, and so it is with Jesus. And here is how we see the example of Jesus, the scarlet cord of His love, running through the Old Testament, an example of His love through this obedient man, Hosea.

Tearing Down Idols

There is nothing about anybody's story that shocks God. There's nothing any one of us has done to stop His redeeming love for you. You may not feel worthy of such love, in the same way Gomer may have not felt worthy of Hosea's love, but He will make sure to let you know in the most personal of ways just how deep His affections are toward you. He desires our commitment, our full attention, our whole hearts, completely surrendered to Him. The idols we make in our hearts? He'll tear them down. We can dress up and play a part, but it won't be long before He asks, "*Aren't you tired? Don't you want to drop off all you're carrying so that you can receive the love I do have for you with open hands?*"

A relationship with Him will challenge us to bare ourselves and open ourselves up to being vulnerable with Him. He knows if you're scared to trust anyone ever again. He knows what's been taken from you or choices you've made that hold you in shame. He's wept for you. True intimacy and vulnerability may be something foreign, and it seems a covenant commitment with Jesus is a big step, so you hesitate. Yet again, He's patient as He lets you discover He is Faithful and True (Rev. 19:11) and He is a safe place to bare all. And even Gomer, a woman scorned and unfaithful, He cleansed and made beautiful—and a bride and a wife.

"I Do"

There were *many* more layers God had to peel back in my heart, but we were going one step at a time. Anytime my heart felt an ache from missing the familiar, or a flashback was triggered, Jesus reminded me He had a plan and a purpose for it all. The enemy may have intended to harm me, but God, who is infinitely wise, can use all things and use them for His glory. "You intended to harm me, but God intended it all for good. He brought me to this position so I could save the lives of many people" (Gen. 50:20, NLT).

Soon after my revelation through Hosea, I attended a special one-night event at a local church near my house. There was a guest speaker, Sheri Rose Shepherd, who shared parts from her book, *His Princess Love Letters,* which God had also used to speak into my identity as His daughter. But there was this new identity, a wife redeemed, stirring in my heart. At the end of the evening, she invited the room to make wedding vows to the Lord, not in a strange way either, but more like making or renewing a covenant commitment with Him. I stood up alongside other women and recited them to Him.

This new idea of Christ as the Bridegroom, that He was my Heavenly Husband and that He'd been providing for me and caring for me, gave me even more security and confidence to follow Him no matter where He led me. These vows solidified even more the deep love I had for Him growing in my heart. And another miracle—my heart felt content in singleness and the desire for an earthly husband was being held at bay for the first time. For the first time I was content being simply His.

"Christ and his spouse are here parting for a while; she must stay below in the gardens on earth,
where she has work to do for him; he must remove to the mountains of spices in heaven,
where he has business to attend for her, as an advocate with the Father.

If a day in his courts be so sweet, what then will an eternity within the veil be!
If this be heaven, O that I were there!"

—Matthew Henry

Part 2—The Project

5

Break My Heart for What Breaks Yours

"Some of you will rebuild the deserted ruins of your cities.
Then you will be known as a rebuilder of walls
and a restorer of homes."
— Isaiah 58:12

As the Lord continued to woo me, He would woo me next by taking me around the world. I always had a yearning to travel, but the cost to go to some of these exotic places always seemed exorbitant and hard to make happen. However, He knows all and created all, and He was about to take me on some grand adventures. After Paris, one of the next adventures God took me on was a mission trip to Haiti. The yearning to travel now matched the yearning to serve God in any way possible. I knew I wanted to spend the rest of my life sharing this good news of what Jesus had done for me with everyone—friends, family, and even strangers. It was too good, too real to keep to myself. I had discovered the best gift on earth, and it was free! All this free gift of salvation required was placing your faith in Jesus and with it came freedom and people's eternal address depended on it.

These yearnings to travel and serve God amounted to me Google-searching overseas mission trips, thinking it would be really convenient if He called me to serve Him in Thailand or somewhere breathtaking like that. My fantasy prone mind was still (and will always be) undergoing construction. I had to do many heart checks to make sure I wasn't pawning off serving God for a mini tropical vacation. While I was a new creation in Christ, I was still being refined daily.

God did the ultimate heart check. *"If you really want to serve me, then go where I want to take you."* I said, "Yes, of course, God. Anywhere!" And where He wanted to take me wasn't the lushness that I imagine Thailand to be, it was Port Au Prince, Haiti, with the missions relief team from my church. That's the opportunity that clearly opened up and the one I had peace about committing to. I was truly excited to go but not so excited when I landed. I was thrown way off upon arriving in this foreign country. Another Paris moment, so to speak. When our team landed, we headed directly for the restrooms. The lights were flickering on and off, at one point going completely dark in a very musty-smelling airport restroom. No sight, no toilet seat, foul smells, pitch-black. God knew what He was doing though. He knew exactly where to put me to prune me. Just like a gardener prunes a rosebush, God was pruning me. He is the Vine Dresser after all, and this is how He produces more spiritual fruit in us (Jn. 15:1–5).

Pruning literally means to cut away dead or overgrown branches to increase fruitfulness and growth, and that's just what He had in mind for me. It was going to take sending me to a third-world country to clip back the thornier parts of my heart. Apparently ten years of neglecting to prune your heart accumulates to a lot of dead brambles and overgrowth.

Being newish to the Christian scene, I kept hearing this familiar Christian phrase from other believers. It was asking God to "break their heart for what breaks His." It sounded very noble, and I prayed it too. Did I fully know what that would mean? No, but He would work with it. I was hearing others share how God broke their hearts for the orphans in slum villages or the homeless population. While yes, these are heartbreaking, I discovered there is another category God's heart breaks for, and it's the thing He broke me free from—those bound in sexual sin, defined by their sexuality, and young minds being shaped to believe that their identity (and even gender) is based on their ever-evolving feelings. When we set people or our feelings on the throne of our hearts, it breaks more than the second Commandment, "Thou shall have no other gods before Me," it breaks God's heart. God's jealous love (Ex. 20:5) is not like the human kind of jealousy. It's more appropriate to say that God is zealous—eager about protecting what is precious to Him, "For I feel a divine jealousy for you, since I betrothed you to one husband, to present you as a pure virgin to Christ (2 Cor. 11:2, ESV). This is coming from the apostle Paul exhorting the Corinthian church.

We choose to give our minds over to depravity, and more than we may realize, we are living out of a poverty-like spiritual state not unlike the poverty I was witnessing all around me in Haiti, and that breaks His heart. To live driven by our carnal impulses makes me think of this C.S. Lewis quote:

> It would seem that Our Lord finds our desires not too strong, but too weak. We are halfhearted creatures, fooling about with drink and sex and ambition when infinite joy is offered us, like an ignorant child who wants to go on making mud pies in a slum because he cannot imagine what is meant by the offer of a holiday at the sea. We are far too easily pleased.

Haiti

What I thought would be a trip filled with serving the local church gladly, helping build wells valiantly actually was a trip filled with establishing even more firmly the call on my life while pruning the old heart and thought patterns. There were tearful phone calls to my mom expressing the selfishness I still felt and how homesick I was. *Pruning.* I was struggling. I was so out of my element. To become a disciple of Jesus, He didn't promise an easy breezy life. He promises abundant life. The requirement of daily dying to self was a lot harder in practice than it was to read about in the Word. I've learned though, that on the other side of these moments of discomfort, we find the most joy. After all, Jesus endured excruciating suffering, and He told His disciples to expect to endure suffering this side of Heaven as well. Sticking through the pain gets you to the moments of glory.

No matter what trials or testing we might face, His presence is always with us, and we can run to that place and find rest for our souls. I had asked Him to let me serve Him. I had asked Him to break my heart for what breaks His. I had asked Him to give me more of the hard and holy things. What did I expect? He was answering, *and* He was with me. His presence was promised, but what wasn't sitting well with me on this trip was that He seemed so far away. I wasn't hearing Him like I heard Him in the comfort of my own home.

I'd brought a travel-sized Bible that felt as foreign to me as the country did. It wasn't my well-worn, well-loved Bible that I had broken in, yet it was still the Word of God. It was something I had to learn then, that even though I didn't *feel* God near (not letting my feelings define absolute truth), that didn't mean He wasn't with me. The truth was the Bible told me He was there (Psalm 16:8), and it was a testing and growing of my faith to press into Him despite how I was feeling. It's so dangerous to let our feelings dictate our lives because feelings are faulty and not reliable. Just as the world is ever-changing, so are feelings. What I was personally going through didn't take away from everything happening all around me. I needed to stand firm on the truth of God's Word, continue on in the daily disciplines of reading His Word, and muting my flesh by letting His Holy Spirit lead me.

As I rose with the crowing of the roosters, I knew there'd be more pruning. My flesh always tempts me to sleep in. But for a week, thanks to the accountability of my team, I would experience in full all that God had for me, that required waking with the sun. I would not be robbed of the blessings this trip had to offer. Some of those blessings? Experiencing the wildest thunderstorms in a city where rain hadn't fallen in months. One of the nights water was pinging off the tin roof that was the makeshift shade covering *on top* of the roof of the building we stayed in. Our team had gone up to pray from that tin-covered rooftop, our voices had to get louder and louder to compete against the rain that began pounding. We prayed for the people of Haiti and for loved ones still without hope. We saw lightning light up the sky and heard the cracking of thunder, with the rain falling even harder. Once the prayer time was over, some of us girls ran inside to grab our shampoo and conditioner to wash our hair because the rain was falling that hard. Haiti's water supply is very scarce and is contaminated, so we hadn't been able to wash our hair in days. *Pruning.*

We laughed as the suds and scent of our shampoo filled the air. I cut and ate a mango for the first time in a kitchen in Haiti. I also cut my finger because I wasn't well trained in slicing slippery fruit with a dull knife. Breakfast, lunch, and dinner consisted of the same meal: rice, beans, and on the rare occasion, cut-up hot dogs. The Haitian women who tended to the kitchen slept in the same room as some of us girls, in bunks covered with mosquito nets, downstairs in what they called "the dungeon" because of the lack of light.

Some of our team put on a vacation Bible school for the neighboring children in a number of different concrete amphitheaters and churches throughout the region, nothing fancy but the fondest memories. I even had the privilege of leading one man to Christ. He followed our team one day as we walked across town from the pastor-training school we were staying at to another school where we would hold one of these vacation Bible schools. He asked why we were there, and I told him to share the Good News that Jesus Christ had died for our sins and had risen to new life and that He offers us this gift of eternal life to those who believe in Him. He asked in a Creole accent, "How do I get this?" and I said, "You just ask Him! And confess you're a sinner in need of a Savior." We sat down on a block wall, I prayed the sinner's prayer, he repeated the words, and just like that he had been forgiven of his sins and had been made right with God and his identity secure in who God says He is: a son, a brother in Christ.

We went to hospitals to pray for the sick babies who had been born with rare illnesses. We prayed with mothers who had just given birth to these babies in rooms with high humidity and no ventilation. It opened my eyes to how blessed most of us really are in the United States, but it also caused me to see why it's so easy for us to forget about God and make ourselves our own gods.

Our team had the opportunity to go to an orphanage and play with the children who lived there, many with severe disabilities who'd been left for dead on the side of roads or in trash bins. Most were confined to wheelchairs. A friend I made on the team taught me to sew right on the spot as we decided to fix holes in a mosquito net that was around a particular crib in the middle of one of the main rooms. There was a baby girl inside who could only lay prostrate, with a tumor the size of a baseball on the right side of her head. She could not move on her own. This meant she could not swipe away the flies that scooted their way through the holes in the net and buzzed around her face. We shooed them all out of the net and stitched fast so they could no longer get through to torment this sweet, precious girl. Jesus sent us right to her.

It might sound beautiful and heroic as I type it now, but it was all so heavy and so much to bear as I was there. I vividly remember another moment in that orphanage. Half the team had taken some of the children outside in their wheelchairs to get some sunlight. I stayed inside with two girls and a boy who were only about 7 or 8 years old. One of the girls and the boy began taunting the other little girl by keeping a ball away from her. The other little girl began crying, crying so hard that tears and snot fell down her face. They just laughed, making fun of her. I couldn't tell them that wasn't nice because I didn't speak their language, which was another really hard barrier to overcome. I couldn't use my words to tell them all the things I wanted to, but rather, I had to show them. I found a rag and sat beside this weeping young girl and began wiping the snot from her nose. She had no motor skills and was unable to get up and wipe on her own.

It was in these moments where I truly felt like the hands of Jesus. This is how He loves us. Through the snot, tears, and foul moments, He comes near. When the annoyances of the enemy irritate us to the point of torment, like flies buzzing and swirling overhead, He stitches up the net and is our Defender. I was reminded how often He'd wiped my tears and snot, and He was using me to show her this same type of love. It was His Spirit that prompted me to do that, to show compassion and serve another instead of serving myself. *Pruning.*

Even after experiencing all that, the spiritual warfare was thick. I felt the enemy right on my heels, trying to steal my joy and replace it with fear and doubt of why I was even there. There were days I was wondering what in the world was wrong with me for not wanting to run to the orphanage and love on all those sweet children another day. My flesh wanted to retreat, my flesh didn't feel comfortable or at home. Most of the girls on the trip were back for their third time, and I couldn't even make it through the first few days. They talked about how their heart broke for that country and the Haitian people. I had to act out of sheer obedience because "this girl" was so out of her comfort zone that playing ball at the orphanage another day was an absolute stretch. *Pruning.*

I wanted my heart to break for these people. I really did. I wanted the dusty and rocky, littered and unpaved roads to feel like home. I wanted to feel called to return to this country with an obvious need, and I just pressed on thinking maybe those feelings would come with time. But the problem was in me comparing my calling to someone else's and allowing my emotions to get the best of me. My calling was something entirely different than theirs, and that's okay. It's actually more than okay, it's necessary. I just didn't know that yet. I was there for a reason far bigger than what my limited mind could comprehend.

America

It wasn't until the middle of that week that I was freed from that deadly temptation to compare myself to those around me and had a breakthrough on what God was *truly* calling me to—advocating for the sanctity of marriage and sharing where our true identity is found.

The Wednesday we were there, I was invited to jump into the bed of one of the trucks with our missions pastor's wife, Mrs. Lore Hooper, whom I've interviewed for the project alongside her husband, Marty Hooper, who led our trip. We were going to run errands around town. I was thrilled to get to explore the surrounding area a bit more as we had only walked a few miles around the compound we were staying at. I felt a relief to be given a different assignment that day. We drove through the city and met a lot of angry stares and were warned not to take our phones out to use our cameras to take photos. Thankfully, there was a counterbalance to those angry stares with Haitian tap-taps (the Haitian version of American taxis) passing by proclaiming, "Jesus is Lord!" and "God is good!" The Bible college and the pastors in training were making a considerable impact on this community. It was evident all around.

As our truck pushed through traffic, the road finally opened up, and the truck was suddenly climbing up the side of a mountain. There were lush greens all around, and I even remember seeing a white dove fly overhead, which in the Bible symbolizes the Holy Spirit. My adventurous spirit awakened. I was enjoying every bit of this refreshing drive to clear my mind. The pastor of the Bible church we had partnered with was the one driving us, and he began to drive our team up this mountain, finally stopping at the very top. We were able to finally get out and stretch our legs.

A few feet away was a ledge that overlooked parts of Haiti, and we were able to see a glimpse of the Caribbean Sea. The chaos we had just driven through looked so calm and serene from way up high. Our friend, we'll call him Pastor B, started pointing out specific areas of Haiti and explaining the epidemics that plague this nation and each region. He recognized that ultimately it's a sin problem, diagnosing not only Haiti but all of humanity as "sin positive" with Jesus as the only anecdote. He was encouraging our team by testifying to all what God was doing within the hearts and minds of the people in Haiti. He shared stories of victory, such as witch doctors who had practiced voodoo for years coming to a saving knowledge of Jesus Christ and being transformed by the work of the Holy Spirit. There were stories of families coming back together that had been broken by the men's habitual infidelity, leaving their women pregnant and left to care for their many children alone. I didn't know it then, but these testimonies he was sharing would be what the heart of the Marriage Project would resemble—testifying to God's faithfulness and a platform to share the testimonies of the once afar off now living for God and stories of broken marriages restored.

It was a solemn tone Pastor B took as he turned to our group and asked, "So how are you guys doing?" By "you guys" he meant the United States of America. He had been the missions pastor at a Southern California church in the US for many years before he felt the call to move to Haiti and start a Bible college there. The answer to that question wasn't a confident, resounding "We're doing great!" It was hesitation mixed with the unfortunate truth that the climate of our country was deteriorating rapidly. Spiritually, physically, mentally, our nation was sick. And this was back in 2014. It's been almost seven years now since that trip, and the confusion, division, and moral depravity has only gotten worse. There was an attack on absolute truth, and a feelings-based doctrine and ideology was spreading. More and more we were seeing the choosing of sides and people living only for themselves or their own truth.

One of the most devastating things is that there's been a division within the church on certain key issues. We are called to love others, yes, but equally as important is the call to hold firm to the truth of God's Word and to be loving to one another. The Bible says, "Your love for one another will prove to the world that you are my disciples" (Jn. 13:35, NLT) and "My children, our love should not be just words and talk; it must be true love, which shows itself in action" (1 Jn. 3:18, NLT). How are we treating each other? Are we calling one another out to repent of sin that's crept in or are we allowing one another to succumb to the climate of the culture? Are we avoiding the hard topics altogether? Are our convictions strong enough?

Pastor B mentioned hearing about some major issues being overturned in the Supreme Court and that "America was in trouble." We are losing, if not already lost, the sacredness of marriage. At the root of this all, I see the same enemy who had it out for me, out to take down the biblical meaning of marriage and the sanctity of it while deceiving people into believing they can live their life the way they want to with no eternal consequence.

Marriage is the very institution God uses to demonstrate His covenant love for His people. We saw that in the Book of Hosea. Why wouldn't the enemy attack the image of the Bride and twist it entirely causing so much hatred and division? In today's world, there can be two brides, no brides or "whatever you want bride to mean" brides. And as long as we're arguing over these things, his work is being done for him.

God speaks plainly on the issue of marriage and it being explicitly between a man and woman. It doesn't matter what I think or say on the matter, it's what His Word tells me. When a nation's idol worship has become sex and a redefinition of marriage, it really is in trouble. It's evident that we are all searching for love (Prov. 19:22), but leaving corrupt man with a corrupt sin nature to define it isn't it. It's helping no one to side on an issue for fairness and the fear of ruffling feathers. We need Jesus more than tolerance. We need Jesus more than political correctness. We simply need Jesus.

It was that statement from Pastor B that startled and troubled me. Deeply. Profoundly. I could not shake it. Similarly to the many lives living in physical poverty in Haiti, many were living in even deeper spiritual poverty in my own backyard—in America. There was an entire generation being fed the same lies I had feasted on through shows, movies, music, and it has gotten even worse with the rise of social media. Here I was extending Christ's love to a nation very much in need of that, but there was a crisis back at home as well. I wanted to go home but with a new charge. I wanted to help God in this work of telling people where an unfailing love could be found and point them to truth no matter what the cost for me.

I knew this message wasn't going to be the most popular. People don't like to be called out on their sin, but that couldn't matter. I'd allowed God to open my heart and eyes to see a great spiritual need—people bound by the sin of sexual immorality and idolatry, and there were even those in the church who were being led astray. I saw the image of the Bride and the sanctity of marriage under siege, and I wanted to throw a life raft out to those being led into enemy territory into those churning waters. People's souls were on the line, and something deep within me broke. I wasn't expecting it, but it was there overlooking the country of Haiti that my heart felt a pang of grief for those who let culture be their god and define truth for them.

My heart broke for America and His prodigal sons and daughters who once knew Him but lost sight of Him in high school or college or who had completely given themselves over to their flesh. I knew firsthand what comes with this territory and letting our desire for love and acceptance rule us. My heart would continue to break anytime I'd be confronted with young girls or young boys, or a girl or guy of any age caught up in a toxic relationship.

My heart broke as I saw the dismantling of marriage and in turn, the family unit, which God designed with a marvelous purpose. When I boarded the plane home from Haiti, I didn't know what to do first or how this would play out. I just knew that I could not back down or shy away from this call. My hope and prayer would be that this message would carry into the next generation that have lived in a world where nothing is clearly defined. I wanted to create something where everything *is* clearly defined and points to God's Word on these matters. I wanted there to be a safe place to land for the young adult girl (or guy) who's been living in shame from past sexual sin or for the one left feeling so empty inside after consuming so much of the secularization of this world. But before this message could be carried out into the world, there was something else the Lord and I would have to work on together first. That would be the call to be brave.

"By standing firm, you will win your souls."

—Luke 21:9

6

The Power of Prayer

"I will make the wilderness a pool of water
and the dry land fountains of water."
— Isaiah 41:18

After coming home from Haiti, I felt called to write. I was being affirmed as a writer and a teacher as I began teaching in the children's ministry at church. Writing is a very vulnerable thing, and you have to be very disciplined. Both of those things were very new to me, and in sharing these really vulnerable parts of myself through writing, I'd have to find courage. The other new thing I would learn in this next season of walking with Jesus was the power in prayer. He was going to teach me to pray because the broken heart would lend to the vision for The Marriage Project. It would be a labor in love, and it would be a labor of prayer.

God would use something personal to teach me what it meant to fervently pray and to build a project on the foundation of those fervent prayers. During this next year, I learned different postures to pray in, when to pray, what to pray, what it meant to let the Holy Spirit lead in prayer, and what it means to listen as I pray. I would pause during those prayer times, grab my journal, and jot down the words that were coming out so passionately so that I wouldn't forget what God was speaking to me and through me as the Holy Spirit prompted. Up until the end of 2015, I felt like a novice when it came to prayer. To do a work for God I had to be ready for a season of prayer and let that be the work first. I was antsy as I was in the beginning phases of learning so many new things such as photography, still traveling and keeping up with Bible study. I just wanted to fast-forward to the part where I was doing something for God and His Kingdom.

Throughout this praying season, I was also reading different books that helped contribute to the fueling of my desire to keep praying for the big things and desires in my heart. Marriage was far from my mind at this point, and being single was still okay with me. I wasn't distracted by a relationship. I took note of many quotes on prayer. I wanted to share a few of my favorites here:

"When the devil sees a man or woman who really believes in prayer, who knows how to pray, and who really does pray, and, above all, when he sees a whole church on its face before God in prayer, he trembles as much as he ever did, for he knows that his day in that church or community is at an end."

—R.A. Torrey

"We are too busy to pray, and so we are too busy to have power. We have a great deal of activity, but we accomplish little; many services but few conversions; much machinery but few results."

—R.A Torrey

"Because you know He can, you can pray with holy confidence."

—Mark Batterson

"Go home. Lock yourself in your room. Kneel down in the middle of the floor, and with a piece of chalk draw a circle around yourself. There, on your knees, pray fervently and brokenly that God would start a revival within that chalk circle."

—Mark Batterson[7]

"Prayer is no petty invention of people, a fancied relief for ills. Prayer is no dreary performance, dead and death dealing. It is God's enabling act for people, living and life giving, joy and joy giving. Prayer is the contact of the soul with God. In prayer, God stoops to kiss us, to bless us, and to aid us in everything that God can devise or we can need. Prayer fills our emptiness with God's fullness. It fills our poverty with God's riches. It exchanges our weaknesses for God's strength. It banishes our littleness with God's greatness. Prayer is God's plan to supply our great and continuous need with God's great and continuous abundance."

—E.M Bounds

---

[7] I have not read any of these books in their entirety apart from *The Circle Maker*. *The Circle Maker* helped me in this season of believing and praying for God to move mightily in my life, but it serves us best to pray and trust that even if God doesn't answer right away or in the affirmative does not mean He hasn't heard or isn't working in our lives. He'll take our desires and work out His best and His will for us in our lives.

Honestly, I had no idea what I was getting myself into, but this is faith. It is one small action or step at a time. This part of the journey was not to a third-world country, it would happen right here at home and right next to my bed by my little bedside table, which became a battleground. The Lord was showing me the fight to win souls was a spiritual battle and to fight spiritual wars, one must fight with spiritual weapons. Ephesians 6:12 tells us, "For we wrestle not against flesh and blood, but against principalities, against powers, against the rulers of the darkness of this world, against spiritual wickedness in high places." My weapons for winning the spiritual battle would be prayer and the Word of God.

In that same year, the urgency to fight for the sanctity of marriage and for the one or ones finding their worth and identity in their sexuality or relationships began to swirl within me. That feeling of urgency turned to action when this arousal of righteous anger toward this sin entered my life in a personal way. A friend I'd met at church confided in me about their struggle with same-sex attraction and came asking for prayer. The first confession of this came when sitting after a church service, a phone call coming through on this friend's phone, and this friend said, "Please pray." This was a phone call from a person this friend had been dating or talking to and was someone that they knew shouldn't be in their life. Did that friend need to answer the phone call? No, but the thing I've come to realize is that sometimes even our best intentions at staying away from the very thing causing us harm is the very thing our flesh runs toward.

However, God's Word tells us there's nothing He allows in our life that's too great for us to handle, "The temptations in your life are no different from what others experience. And God is faithful. He will not allow the temptation to be more than you can stand. When you are tempted, he will show you a way out so that you can endure"

(1 Cor. 10:13, NLT). God always gives us a way out of temptation. We are faced with a choice.

It's A Battle Royale and It's Real

I can recall a moment during this year, 2015, when I was tempted to go somewhere I knew I didn't really need to be. I started to drive home but pulled off the freeway and parked. I contemplated in my mind what I was going to do, keep going home or turn back and hang a little longer with some people I rarely saw and really missed. If we take the time to think carefully enough, we can see where the choice will land us. We're not called to be perfect and never sin. We will never be sinless in this life, but as we know Jesus and His Word more and more, we will desire to sin deliberately less and less. But even in those moments of weakness, and when we slip, I don't believe He is angry. I imagine a look of compassion toward us when we make mistakes when He knows we truly desire to make changes. One of my favorite Scriptures is, "How can I know all the sins lurking in my heart? Cleanse me from these hidden faults. Keep your servant from deliberate sins! Don't let them control me. Then I will be free of guilt and innocent of great sin. May the words of my mouth and the meditation of my heart be pleasing to you, O LORD, my rock and my redeemer" (Ps. 19:12–14, NLT). When this is our prayer and our heart's posture, He honors this and helps us to keep walking.

We sin everyday—hidden sins, hidden faults that we are unaware of before the Holy Spirit points them out—but it's the deliberate sin that needs adjusting and deep convictions that can't be ignored. Deliberate sin is when we know what's true, when we know what's wrong, and we forge on anyway and don't turn back or don't turn our hearts to say "sorry" to Him if we do mess up. Pride develops here. It's dangerous. In my case, I didn't go home. I chose to go hang a little longer, and I didn't do anything I would later regret, but by hanging a little longer, old feelings surfaced, and then I had to hand it all back over to the Lord all over again and work through fresh heart pains. I asked a friend to hold me accountable, and she did. She helped me navigate through those next few days.

And I saw that in the case of this aforementioned friend who answered the phone when they knew they shouldn't. There was a confession to me, which was a start, yet there was still a deliberate disobedience happening where sin was not being rightly dealt with. I could see the battle raging for this friend's affections. I could see the turmoil and the anguish on this friend's face and that there was a sense of powerlessness prevailing. They were letting their feelings take over.

The battle that was evident to me was confirmed by this friend as they opened up more and described this as an inner war going on. While this friend believed the Word of God and their conscience was telling them the true thing, simultaneously their feelings were tempting them to do the exact opposite of what they knew to be right. Confusion and compromise happen here. Intermingled with our debased thoughts comes the hissing whisper of the devil and it can drown out all reason. And his goal is to have us give into it because he knows shame immediately follows it. This is how Satan operates. Temptation to gratify the flesh with the promise of liberation, but what follows is a tighter shackle to our sin and overwhelming guilt. Your identity is now under attack, and you may be labeled as something that you're absolutely not, yet you get so deep in, you begin to believe the titles for yourself and live them out accordingly. Labeling anyone as anything other than "wonderfully and fearfully made by God" stirs unrest within me. Labels sound so definitive, and you start believing something that is based on a lie.

During this time in my life I would also become a substitute teacher for a short period of time. I walked into some junior high classrooms with fresh eyes and no knowledge of who these kids were. I later found out, there were a few targeted as "trouble kids." A few hours spent with them, and I could have guessed that, but I didn't know their history. They were always sent out of the classroom because they were misbehaving. But what if they were misbehaving because they were always told they were the trouble kids and they just started to believe it and were acting the part? I determined in my heart to not send them out of the classroom and instead wanted to call out something in them they were gifted at. I was looking for the redeeming quality. One of them was a really good artist. Okay, so maybe he was avoiding doing his math homework and what he was drawing was questionable—but guess what? I saw a subtle change in him over the course of the time I spent with him because I complimented him instead of labeling him as trouble. Will he stop stirring up trouble? Not necessarily. But at least he heard one encouraging thing spoken over his life, and I prayed that he would one day know Jesus and use his talents for good and for the Kingdom. In this same way, God calls out the best in us and has spoken words over us and our identities, and that's what's true. Doing anything once or twice or a hundred times does not define your personhood.

Now, it's clear in the Bible that sin is sin and not one sin is greater than another. But the Bible does speak directly about sexual immorality. Romans 1:24–32 reads:

> "So God abandoned them to do whatever shameful things
> their hearts desired. As a result, they did vile and degrading
> things with each other's bodies. They traded the truth about
> God for a lie. So they worshiped and served the things God
> created instead of the Creator himself, who is worthy of

eternal praise! Amen. That is why God abandoned them to their shameful desires. Even the women turned against the natural way to have sex and instead indulged in sex with each other.

And the men, instead of having normal sexual relations with women, burned with lust for each other. Men did shameful things with other men, and as a result of this sin, they suffered within themselves the penalty they deserved. Since they thought it foolish to acknowledge God, he abandoned them to their foolish thinking and let them do things that should never be done. Their lives became full of every kind of wickedness, sin, greed, hate, envy, murder, quarreling, deception, malicious behavior, and gossip. They are backstabbers, haters of God, insolent, proud, and boastful. They invent new ways of sinning, and they disobey their parents.

They refuse to understand, break their promises, are heartless, and have no mercy. They know God's justice requires that those who do these things deserve to die, yet they do them anyway. Worse yet, they encourage others to do them, too."

Sexual sin is the only sin against one's own body (1 Cor. 6:18), and there are reasons God has boundaries around such an intimate, erotic thing. Boundaries means someone loves you enough to tell you "no" for your own good. There are many verses that address sexual sin head on, if you'd care to look them up and read them: 1 Corinthians 6:13; 1 Thessalonians 4:3; 1 Corinthians 6:9; 1 Corinthians 10:8; Galatians 5:19; Jude 1:7; Revelation 9:21; Matthew 5:32; Revelation 2:21; Mark 7:21; 2 Corinthians 12:21;

Ephesians 4:19; 1 Peter 4:2; Romans 13:13. Just as God created marriage, He created sex. He created it with purpose and passion—and with boundaries. However, left up to a sinful humanity, we see how far from its original design it can go.

"Do You Want to Get Well?"

This suffering within (Rom. 1:27) was evident in my friend's despair and plea for relief. Any time this friend would ask for prayer, I was grieved, and I would pray. My prayers were fiery, and I can only attribute that to how fiery God's heart was on this matter. My prayers weren't the quick halfhearted kind but were prayers that I spoke out loud with my heart beating in my chest. I sensed the Holy Spirit moving for this friend and who this friend represented. It wasn't just one prayer but continued prayer and fasting for these chains to be broken. There were days words weren't even enough to express the anguish I felt, tears would just fall out of my eyes leaving my Bible or journal pages wet, and sorrow from the deepest part of me came forth causing me to just gasp for air at some points.

It was not my own courageousness that kept this sort of prayer going but the Holy Spirit's power that kept me praying and friends He sent in alongside to pray with me as well. We even all set the alarm on our phones to 6:18 p.m. for a period of time to remind us to all pray in unity. The 6:18 came from Ephesians 6:18, "And pray in the Spirit on all occasions with all kinds of prayers and requests. With this in mind, be alert and always keep on praying for all the Lord's people."

As these prayers continued, I saw God working firsthand, and I witnessed prayers being answered in astounding ways. My recurring thought through it all was, "Wow, prayer really works!" and also "How deep the Father's love for us." He loves us all so much and wants everyone to be His. He created us to be with Him forever and wants not one soul to depart from Him or spend eternity separated from Him. Hell was not created for us but for Satan and the legion of fallen angels that fell with him. "Then the King will turn to those on the left and say, 'Away with you, you cursed ones, into the eternal fire prepared for the devil and his demons'" (Matt. 25:41, NLT). What lands anyone there in the afterlife would be to blaspheme the Holy Spirit (the unpardonable sin) by refusing to ever declare "Jesus as Lord" and refusing to repent of their sin.

I don't take that lightly. If anyone blatantly refuses to turn to Him, He will not force them to be with Him. I just read something in Scripture that backs that up. It's found in John 5. Jesus asked a man who'd been sick for 38 years a question you think would be an obvious "yes." Jesus approached him and asked, "Would you like to get well?" That really struck me. Jesus gave him a choice. Not everyone wants to get well. When it comes to our physical well-being, we would not refuse that offer. When it comes to our spiritual well-being, why is that answer not the same resounding "yes"?

One of the beautiful things about the discipline of praying is that not only do we get to partner with God for the ones being prayed for, but it brings the one praying nearer to God and it changes the one praying. Prayer was breaking things in me that were *still* strongholds in *my* heart and mind. I made memories with the Lord no one can take away, and I know Him even more intimately because of this season. I know how much power there truly is in prayer because of how I saw God move during this time.

I mentioned learning different postures in prayer, and you may have been thinking, "Huh?" Well, what I meant was there is no rigidity in how you pray. There was one I like to call the "face down surrender," meaning I'd literally get down, face to the ground, and pray. Try it. I know, it may sound weird, but just try it. In that humbling posture, I was inclined to certain thoughts I'd never been inclined to before. God saw my heart posture over my physical posture, I was in submission to His Lordship in my life, and He spoke to me and answered things very clearly. He led me to pray for the senses of the people He put on my heart. I prayed for their "sight," what they were "hearing," and "touch"—down to their fingertips as in what they were scrolling through.

One of my closest friends and I committed to a week of fasting from sleep (not completely but waking up at 4:00 a.m. every day for a week) to pray. There were days I would have failed miserably had it not been for her phone call at 4:00 a.m. to wake me up, to pray on the phone together. Our voices may have sounded sleepy, but again, God doesn't need perfection but a willingness. One night we spent the night together, so we were in person for this prayer time. Early that morning (3:30 a.m.), I was lying there half-asleep, half-awake, and a verse came to my mind, "Submit yourselves, then, to God. Resist the devil, and he will flee from you" (Jm. 4:7). Just then, my cell phone screen lit up, and a push notification came through from an app I had on my phone. And wouldn't you know it, James 4:7 flashed before my eyes. I woke up my friend to show her. We felt encouraged that God put that verse on my heart and confirmed He was there through that verse popping up. We needed that encouragement because we wanted to sleep through instead of push through.

We got up, got down on the floor, put on worship music, and began to pray. My friend suddenly had this overwhelming sense of not feeling worthy enough to pray and shared she was feeling that the Lord would answer my prayers but not hers. This was a blatant attack from the enemy who hates prayer (see prayer quotes I listed earlier). If he couldn't overcome us through the temptation to fall back asleep, he'd attack her thoughts. We spoke the James 4:7 verse out, resisting him, banking on that promise that as we drew near to God, he would flee. As we prayed through, we realized this feeling of unworthiness was an insight into the very person's thoughts whom we were fasting and praying for. How the feeling of unworthiness keeps any of us from approaching a holy God because the devil would want us to believe we don't deserve the sort of love that Christ offers and that our sin is too great to ever be forgiven. That is absolutely untrue.

That very same day, we heard from the friend we'd been praying for. We hadn't heard from that particular friend in months. My jaw dropped. We were amazed at the timing, the tangible proof that God heard us and was working.

Pools of Water, River of Life

It was about eight months into the year, and I went from those prayers in the wee hours of the morning, to praying prayers on long drives, to praying on walks, really praying "whenever the heaviness was too much to bear" prayers. Yet in the eighth month of this year my prayers and eyes started to feel dry, like I had nothing left to give. I felt burnt out and like there were no tears left to shed. As I came to the spot beside my bed, I just lay there curled up on the floor feeling tired. My wall held evidence that I'd been there and that much prayer had happened. I had a wall full of hot pink and highlighter orange Post-its tacked to the wall with names of people I loved circled, things revealed to me in those prayer moments, praise reports, and promises from Scripture on display so I could look at them and hold onto all the Lord had revealed to me.

As I lay there on my floor, I breathed out. I closed my eyes and saw in my vision on this journey with Jesus we were now in a dry desert. We had left the shore, the forest, and clearing far behind. I saw myself (still in my white dress) propping my foot up on a shovel I'd sunk into the ground. I stopped to wipe the sweat from my brow. Across the wide-open desert were holes spanning out beyond the horizon. With every prayer, had I dug a hole? "I couldn't have prayed that many prayers," I thought. And then a new thought—perhaps some of those holes had been prayers previously prayed by others, for their loved ones, the prodigal sons and daughters. What did the holes even mean? I lifted my head up and opened my Bible. I "just so happened" to turn right to 2 Kings 3:16, and this verse opened the floodgates of tears that had seemingly dried up. "...This is what the LORD says: 'This dry valley will be filled with pools of water!'" (2 Kings 3:16). These holes would be filled and be made *pools* of water! He made a promise to me through that strong word, "will." I learned that anywhere in the Bible you read Him speak, "I AM..." ("I am going to do a new thing" in Isaiah 43:19) or "I will," He is making a promise. This promise helped me see I wasn't laboring in vain and my prayers were helping to plow up soil in hard-soiled hearts. And the water that would fill these hearts would be the Living Water, Jesus Christ, who fills our once-hollowed-out hearts to overflowing. There would be pools of Living Water in hearts of new believers who were dying of thirst, panting under the weight of their sin through what He would call me to do.

If You Only Knew What God Has for You

Jesus calls Himself the Living Water, "But whoever drinks the water that I give him will never be thirsty again. But the water that I give him will become in him a spring of water [satisfying his thirst for God] welling up [continually flowing, bubbling within him] to eternal life" John 4:14, AMP; "Jesus stood up and cried out, 'If anyone thirsts, let him come to me and drink. Whoever believes in me, as the Scripture has said, 'Out of his heart will flow rivers of living water'" (Jn. 7:37–38, ESV).

Just like Jesus met a Samaritan woman at a well, in the heat of the day, so He meets us in the driest times in our lives, in the heat of the day and offers us a drink that will satisfy the thirst we have been trying to quench. Jesus answered this woman who'd had five husbands and was in a relationship with another man who was not her husband, "'If only you knew the gift God has for you and who you are speaking to, you would ask me, and I would give you living water.' 'Sir,' the woman said, 'You have nothing to draw with and the well is deep. Where can you get this living water?' Jesus answered, 'Everyone who drinks this water will be thirsty again, but whoever drinks the water I give them will never thirst. Indeed, the water I give them will become in them a spring of water welling up to eternal life'" (Jn. 4:10– 14, NIV).

"Drink water from your own well —
share your love only with your wife.
Why spill the water of your springs in the streets,
having sex with just anyone?
You should reserve it for yourselves.
Never share it with strangers."

— Proverbs 5:16–17

7

Born to Be Born Again

"I will say to the prisoners, 'Come out in freedom,'
and to those in darkness, 'Come into the light.'"
— Isaiah 49:9

Culture will argue that people are "just born a certain way," and I agree. We're all born with a selfish, self-gratifying nature. I can understand the sentiment behind the idea that you are doing the most loving thing when you accept people as they live out who *they* believe they truly are or were born to be. However, I want to counter that and take a stance on the side of it being the most unloving thing.

The argument of being born any sort of way falls short when the Lord showed me we are not to remain as we are—born in our carnal, earthly frame of minds—but He tells us we must be born again. To experience abundant life, it's important to understand this concept. I didn't fully understand it until I was baptized. It was so freeing to come up out of that water feeling washed, clean from my sin. Like the feeling of taking a shower after a really hard, long day, so it is coming to Jesus, a shower for our souls.

It is the most freeing thing to find our identity in Him and resting in that. But we must address the idols in our hearts first. Our hearts are prone to make idols, and those idols can come in many forms—finding love, our emotions, our phones, our rights, our own definition of love, ourselves, even marriage. An idol is anything we elevate above God in our hearts. It's good to take inventory of what we are making our life's passion and goal and ask ourselves whether it is elevating and honoring God or ourselves more. Are we truly living out His commandments and choosing to die to our flesh and its desires or are we indulging? Our hearts cannot be trusted. There's a verse in the book of Jeremiah that really shows us the depth of deceit into which we are all born, "The heart is more deceitful than all else and is desperately sick; who can understand it?" (Jer. 17:9, NASB).

Let's call once more on the wise Matthew Henry to explain this more in depth:

> It is true in general, there is that wickedness in our hearts which we ourselves are not aware of and do not suspect to be there; it is a common mistake among the children of men to think themselves, their own hearts at least, a great deal better than they really are. The heart, the conscience of man, in his corrupt and fallen state, is deceitful above all things.

> It calls evil good and good evil, puts false colors upon things, and cries peace to those to whom peace does not belong. When men say in their hearts that there is no God, or he does not see, or he will not require, or they shall have peace though they go on; and a thousand similar suggestions the heart is deceitful. It cheats men into their own ruin; and this will be the aggravation of it, that they are self-deceivers, self-destroyers. Herein the heart is desperately wicked; it is deadly, it is desperate.

Born of the Spirit

The Bible records a very specific encounter in the gospel of John between one of the religious leaders (who as a group were out to kill Jesus) and Jesus when he walked among men over 2,000 years ago. This man, Nicodemus, clearly demonstrates that his conscience had been pricked as he heard Jesus teach because He wanted to hear just a little more of what Jesus had to say, especially on the topic of what it meant to be born again. Because this man had a reputation to uphold as a firm antagonist to Jesus's ministry, he went to visit Jesus under the cover of night. Being seen with Jesus would have ruined his reputation with the other Pharisees. Nicodemus acknowledged that Jesus was a teacher who had come from God, "For no one can do these signs that you do unless God is with him" (Jn. 3:2, ESV).

"Yet Jesus replied, 'I tell you the truth, unless you are born again, you cannot see the Kingdom of God.' Nicodemus said to him, 'How can a man be born when he is old? Can he enter a second time into his mother's womb and be born?' Jesus answered, 'Truly, truly, I say to you, unless one is born of water and the Spirit, he cannot enter the kingdom of God. That which is born of the flesh is flesh, and that which is born of the Spirit is spirit. Do not marvel that I said to you, "You must be born again." The wind blows where it wishes, and you hear its sound, but you do not know where it comes from or where it goes. So it is with everyone who is born of the Spirit'" (Jn. 3:3–8, ESV).

I'm going to quote one more Bible teacher that I have learned so much from, Oswald Chambers. He sheds a bit more light on the new birth Nicodemus was so puzzled over. He states this, "The new life manifests itself in conscious repentance and unconscious holiness... this new birth gives a power of vision whereby I begin to discern God's rule. His rule was there all the time, but true to His nature; now that I received His nature I can see His rule."[8]

Being born of the spirit is a re-sensitization to the senses, specifically sight. This new birth gives sight to those once blind to God and the things of His Kingdom. We could all say we were born a certain kind of way, yet what the Bible teaches is that to inherit the Kingdom of God we must be born of the Spirit, born again. It's no wonder we are not satisfied with that fragile, feelings-based identity and are always grasping for more. You may feel "free" for a period of time for stepping into what you feel is your true identity, but time will tell this won't be enough. We were not born to be satisfied in our sin state or living impurely. We were born to bring glory to God our Creator, and until our identity is found in Him, any counterfeit identity will come up short.

I hear of individuals who undergo surgeries to change their gender and they make all the changes they believe will cause soul rest and happiness. Yet I've heard testimonies of individuals later in life state that was still not enough. They are left feeling even more isolated, even more incomplete, and *that* breaks my heart.

My mom and dad have seen me from the start, from the day I was born. They knew me and loved me. They loved my pure sense of joy and laughter despite my tantrums and selfish pouty glares. In that same way, God sees each one of us, no matter what age, in that same childlike light. He saw us in our mother's womb (Ps. 139:13), and He knows who He created you to be. He's made a way to reconcile us back to Himself, and that way leads us back to purity, causing us to see like we've never seen before or like we once did as a child. As we are called to Him and we respond, we are born of the Spirit and into a new nature—putting on Christ's nature as we receive Him.

---

[8] This is from an amazing daily devotional, *My Utmost for His Highest* by Oswald Chambers.

"...Put on the new self, which in the likeness of God has been created in righteousness and holiness of the truth. And have put on the new self who is being renewed to a true knowledge according to the image of the One who created him. Do you not know that you are a temple of God and that the Spirit of God dwells in you? But whoever drinks of the water that I will give him shall never thirst; but the water that I will give him will become in him a well of water springing up to eternal life" (Eph. 4:24; Col. 3:10; 1 Cor. 3:16; Jn. 4:14). We are not called to be born again to go on sinning or living according to our own truth or to our liking. No, we are to be born again so that we can testify to the One who has the power to redeem and restore what the locusts have eaten (Jl. 2:25–32).

The Bridal World

I was propelled into the world of photography, which became a specialization in wedding photography. The girl who once made it her life's goal to find her husband was now photographing weddings for a living and wasn't bitter. I was filled with joy in getting to do this work. I was gifted a camera the Christmas of 2013 (after the music festival, a couple of months into Bible study) and before leaving for Haiti. I had no idea what I was doing handling this big, bulky piece of equipment and certainly felt unqualified. I just kept saying "yes" to friends asking me to take portraits for them, and I learned even more lessons in trusting God along the way. I had no experience working with a digital camera, and I remember feeling overwhelmed at all the fancy buttons and menu options. It was sheer grace that one day a switch in my brain just flipped on and I understood how the ISO intertwined with the other two crucial settings needed to confidently shoot in manual mode. Being able to shoot on manual mode meant I could believe that I was getting somewhere, and I could maybe, one day, call myself a professional.

Right after my photography website launched, I volunteered to help another photographer at a bridal expo at a booth of hers. I thought it would be a great way to gain experience and become immersed in the bridal world, learning how I could contribute to the wedding photography niche in the industry. Around lunchtime, I took a break and began scoping out the other vendor booths. There were so many details to the wedding planning business. Florists, videographers, venues, bridesmaids and groomsmen attire, and of course one of the main vendors is the dress shops. Bridal gown boutiques had their booths set up for potential brides to stop at and browse their collection. I wondered how many brides and grooms walking around even understood the weight of such a big commitment. As I began to second-shoot for other wedding photographers, I saw so many different types of weddings, and a lot of them left God out of the picture. I understand there are all types of wedding ceremonies and traditions, but to make such a weighty decision and vow to one another without acknowledging a higher authority made me ponder what that would mean for their future. What would I have wanted to know before getting married? Was marriage everything they imagined it would be? Was it something entirely different? After a few years of marriage did they feel they were drifting away from each other? Would having an individual relationship with God first help keep a marriage together?

The Marriage Project

The concept of The Marriage Project was birthed at my friend's baby shower, celebrating the near arrival of her son. It was smack-dab the middle of summer, and I was smack-dab in the middle of that intense prayer year. It was super humid and hot in southern California, which is a bit unusual for our typical dry desert climate. I found myself in a beautiful indoor setting, attempting to stay cool surrounded by admirable examples of women, all in a season of momma-hood and wifehood. As I sat back and enjoyed each one of their conversations, I was inspired by their ability to talk freely and openly about their struggles of juggling life, marriage, and the raw honesty in how things were really going at home. My single-girl ears perked up because I thought it would be so helpful to hear what these women in an entirely different season of life were walking through.

Up until that point, I had zero relationship experience outside of the two very toxic earlier relationships, but I had a camera and I had time. If I aspired to be a wife one day, hearing from other leading ladies in the thick of it might contribute to marital success in the future. My job allowed me contact with brides-to-be and their fiancés. I didn't really get to experience their relationship past the wedding day. Being single, the whole marriage thing was foreign to me apart from hearing sermons on the topic of marriage or the few marriage counseling books I'd picked up and skimmed through. I never had really even thought about it before. I didn't even know what it meant to think about God's design for marriage or that it had a divine purpose.

I thought it might be pretty cool to reach out to a couple of these new friends to see whether they'd ever want to do a photo shoot, thinking documenting their marriage and telling their story would be something that hasn't been done by many or even at all. I wanted to showcase the beauty of a Christ-centered marriage along with the testimonies of these couples. If their stories were affecting me, how much more would they be helpful for a girl similar to me who wanted to believe for marriage but had a lot of scars and relationship baggage to work through.

Along with sharing my testimony, maybe the sharing of their testimony would reach a heart in a way mine couldn't. It would help prepare them for the future they had always dreamt of but didn't know how to attain. If I've learned one thing, marriage is hard work. It's hard enough with having God at the center of it, how much harder and grueling and heartbreaking with God not at the center? It was a progression in realizing this speaking up for marriage and highlighting couples' stories could speak to the ones God had been breaking my heart for, those on a destructive path, and maybe this was the very reason He had begun to break my heart in the first place. These stories could protect young girls vulnerable to idolizing marriage and the fantasy of the perfect prince and the white horse. That wasn't the only thing to live for. These stories could be the voice to speak to the ones lost and confused in a lost and confusing world wondering why someone would even want to get married at all.

The imagery could be the way to magnify the image of Christ's Bride, the Church, together in one place testifying of His presence in their lives. These stories could take someone's identity crisis head on and bring God the glory for all the work He'd done in their lives and given them their firm and secure identities, which weren't found in their significant other. This project could display the beauty and complexity of marriage and how bringing Jesus into the picture changed everything.

What if God was just waiting for someone to proclaim "that true love isn't defined by the world but that love is defined by the One who laid down His life to redeem the world"? Perhaps this proclamation and project could serve to purify the Church, His bride, and call her to repent and draw once more from the water of His well. What if God was just waiting for us to be "the church that knows the heart of her King and does not fear conflict with the world but rather, she embraces the conflict as His vehicle to radical transformation." What if?

Testimonies Behind the Matrimonies

A week after the baby shower I was dreaming up photo shoot ideas and praying for the right timing for this project to begin. I didn't want to go ahead of God in this, and I wanted to make sure this was His heart and His project. So I prayed and waited. I reached out to a couple of the women who were at the baby shower, but with kids and husbands and life happening, finding time in their schedule for a photo shoot was tricky. I didn't want to make anything happen prematurely because I firmly believe there's a time to wait on the Lord and a time to act. Just like Zechariah 4:6 says, "It is not by force nor by strength, but by my Spirit', says the Lord of Heaven's Armies" and that was how I would know if and when this new idea was to be carried out.

I felt God gave me the tagline for this project, *Testimonies Behind the Matrimonies*, as a sort of wordplay to describe what I was doing when I first began. But then it stuck. It summed it all up so nicely. So what is a testimony you may be thinking? Well, let me offer a definition from Merriam Webster's dictionary.

tes·ti·mo·ny:

1 a: "a solemn declaration usually made orally by a witness under oath..."
b: "firsthand authentication of a fact"

: EVIDENCE
c: an outward sign

2 a: "an open acknowledgment"
b: "a public profession of religious experience"

3 a: "the tablets inscribed with the Mosaic law (2): the ark containing the tablets
b: "a divine decree attested in the Scriptures"

I love what one of the sentence examples in the dictionary uses to describe "testimony"—"the personal *testimonies* of survivors of the war". That war? I've already mentioned it, it's the war that's been declared on marriage as a whole, on marriages, and on your identity. What this project really would be are some stories from survivors of that war because they have placed their hope in the ultimate Victor, Jesus Christ.

Think about this: if the devil has declared war on you, yet Jesus has defeated the devil through His death on the cross and resurrecting from the grave to give us new life, when we side with Jesus, that ultimately makes us the victors as well. These couples have risen against all odds and stand to proclaim the glory of their God. All of the testimonies shared in the project are outward proclamations of an inward change in an individual person. These testimonies are confirmation to how God has redeemed and reclaimed not just my story but many others' stories. Sharing testimonies is powerful evidence to God's healing power that still happens today.

Some argue in today's world that if God were to perform the same miracles He did in the Old or New Testament that they'd believe in Him, miracles such as turning water into wine, making blind men see, bushes burning, raining manna down from heaven, and so forth. Yet as I hear from the people He's radically changed (we're talking former atheists, drug dealers, and mob bosses), this proves to me that He's still in the miracle-working business. How can you account for a radically changed life apart from Christ? You don't hear of it.

Speaking of our culture in today's America, this war is literally at our fingertips, on our phones. This war is whatever is fighting to claim your precious time and winning, it's whatever has a stronghold on you. It's the thing you want to quit but can't. It's the person you know isn't contributing to your well-being, but you can't seem to break it off. Between Internet pornography dismantling marriages and ruining lives to the use of social media feeding into our growing dissatisfaction with how our lives look, the enemy is wreaking havoc in homes and lives. What I've learned through this all is that marriage looks less like an "Instagram worthy feed" and a lot more like blood, sweat, and tears.

If we aren't careful, we can forget this and get caught up in the "Instagram worthy" photos dancing before our eyes whenever we enter an app on our phone. As a photographer, I see a lot of this and have been caught in this comparison trap. And while photography is an important part of my journey with God and another part of this project, I wanted to get past the superficial picture posting and get to the heart of marriages.

Photographs were always meant to capture certain moments in time, and for each of these couples I wanted to give them a stone of remembrance, photos that would serve as flags to put down in the soil on the mound of their marital victories. I wanted them to look back on the photos and remember what they were fighting for as they fight for their marriage and their family. The photos would be included to put faces to names for listeners who could search the accompanying site after but the significance would go far deeper than that. These photos ought to be blown up, framed, and lining the hallways of Heaven. These are the kings and queens of Heaven after all. Royalty. Redeemed. The vision that began as a photography project bloomed into the idea of a podcast. The podcast idea was so that listeners can *hear* from couples I've interviewed and listen to the stories—eyes *and* ears open to hear from God's heart. A friend confirmed this idea when she told me she had just heard a lyric from a favorite song, "Our weapon will be our sound," and that sounded exactly like what I had in mind, a battle cry to spread hope.

Eyes of Faith

Jesus said to Nicodemus, the religious leader who had asked him what it meant to be born again, "I assure you, we tell you what we know and have seen, and yet you won't believe our testimony" (Jn. 3:11, NLT). So a project telling others what we know and have seen? Yet Jesus's words hit me, would anyone even listen, let alone believe? Could they? It is important to note the story of Nicodemus and his asking about being reborn. There has to be a moment where your heart asks Jesus to open the eyes of your heart so you can see the things unseen. Even with telling of what we have known and seen, stories like these can only be seen, heard and understood with new eyes and new ears. This would be the time to pause and ask Him to help you see, to help you desire to change. There's no time better than now to ask Him to see the things of His Kingdom and to help you out of the place you've been stuck for quite some time.

The stories I've documented aren't the classic love stories of a favorite TV show or movie. They are the real stories of couples who have found that fulfillment in life doesn't even come from marriage or each other. It's about discovering God as your First Love. Not even marriage will satisfy the deepest longings within. That was news to me, but it's what I'd been understanding and learning as He made Himself more and more known to me through His Word. It's

Him and Him alone that will meet you right where you are, today, in any hurt, in any fear, or in any pain. I encourage you to practice talking to Him first, right now. Then journey on...

"Marriage exists most ultimately to display the covenant-keeping love between Christ and his church."

—John Piper

8

Oregon Calling

"The wilderness and the land will be glad; the desert will rejoice
and blossom like a rose."
—Isaiah 35:1

O regon called me, literally. It showed up on my caller ID. The
phone call wasn't important, but I knew it was God calling
me there. As I was learning the photography ropes, I had been con-
templating going to a photography conference in Portland, Oregon,
but had no one to go with, so I was a bit hesitant. I chose to take
the call ID as confirmation, and I drove by myself up the California,
Pacific Northwest coast until 17 hours later I landed myself in
Portland, Oregon, for the very first time.

I had so much uninterrupted time alone with God on the drive.
I remember one moment, turning a corner and having a wide-open
road with a tall mountain covered in evergreens in front of me, and
I could imagine Jesus atop that mountain. Here's what I wrote in
my journal about that experience and another story from the Bible
that blew me away.

> I read about Enoch and his walk with God. I pictured this as
> a literal walk, side by side, commenting and complimenting

God on the beauty of the sunrise (up before the sun). The part that hit me was that he gave God his undivided attention. As he spent more and more time with Him, he gained a greater and greater understanding of the depth of who He is. He allowed fewer and fewer interruptions until there were none at all and his walk of faith became actual sight. He was brought into the presence of the LORD (GEN. 5:21–24), literally. He departed the earth, never dying but being caught up with God. I think of my drive to Oregon. I was alone with God for 8 or 9 hours at one point. I genuinely felt myself drawing closer and closer to Him, I will never forget the vision of Jesus standing atop a mountain I was driving toward. I saw Him, heard Him, and felt Him in new ways. The interruptions were becoming fewer and fewer. Then I got out of my car, the trip was over, and interruptions came flooding in. Text messages, social media, conversations about my trip. It's almost like we've almost made it into the fullness of His presence and then we fall victims to our flesh and distractions once more.

That uninterrupted time with God was such a gift, and it's amazing how in tune we really can become with His Spirit when we cut out all of life's distractions. All my life had led up to this point, and the adventures God was continuing to invite me to be on were nothing short of amazing. This was another test in the call to be brave, to have the courage to not just go solo and sit in the back of a first Bible study meeting but to drive solo for such a long distance. This was most definitely to be training ground for what still was ahead.

The City of Roses

That first trip to Portland served its purpose, more calling me out of my comfort zone (pruning still in process) and to expand my capacity for what I could mentally, physically, spiritually handle. I had my own idea about who God wanted me to interview for this marriage project, but He had other plans. The vision was bigger than what I even imagined (Eph. 3:20).

The beginning of 2017 was marked by letting go of a few more dreams I had held tightly onto, one being when he would bring my husband. The singleness was wearing on me a bit. I thought life with God would mean Him immediately bringing me a husband. I just kept waiting for that part to happen, but He kept holding it at bay. There was a project He had for me to begin first. Fast-forward to July of 2017. One of my good friends invited me to go with her to Portland, simply to be a travel buddy and support as she was traveling there to be in her mom's wedding. I'd been experiencing a lull in my photography bookings and didn't have much work that summer. I wasn't quite sure what it all meant. I knew that if God wanted to, there would be an outpouring of wedding inquiries in my inbox and speedy bookings. But that's not what was happening, and I was disappointed. I thought I should be growing in this business since this was my second year doing it full-time.

The silence in my inbox had me reevaluating what exactly I was supposed to do with my summer and career. Was it His grace extending some much-needed rest after a whirlwind start to the year? Perhaps. In hindsight, I believe it was to allow me to shift my focus off my photography business and onto this project because He had some people for me to meet who had some pretty awesome stories to share, thus kickstarting The Marriage Project into high gear. Here's how my brain was working in those May and June months leading up to our July trip: "Maybe I should use my fashion degree and get some fashion editorial work in my portfolio?" "What companies should I reach out to?" "Maybe I should…maybe I should do…" I was so sure fashion photography was the direction I was supposed to go, so much so that I redesigned my website to look more like a resume. I reached out to a few companies I would want to work with. I got one initial reply, and after my response back to that email, nothing. The few others I sent out? Crickets. I'll admit I was getting even more frustrated, discouraged, and fighting waves of doubt. Thank God for the support system He places in our lives — the circle of friends and family who are in your corner, who believe in you more than you believe in yourself and pick you up with words of encouragement and help with some creative ideas to hold you over until God pulls back the curtain of the grand reveal. I call them my "fortress" and God, the Ultimate Fortress. He did not let me get mixed up in any work He hadn't called me to.

One of those friends suggested I follow a social media account called Christian Women in Business. This account is the very instrument God used to connect me to what and who He had waiting for me in Oregon. There had been a post posing this question: "What makes a great business idea?" I noticed one of the comments in the comment thread that caught my attention. She wrote that God had given her an idea for a business that would thrive, but she also shared she had patiently waited 7 years, believing God would fulfill His vision He had given her in His time.

I clicked over to her website and saw a beautiful display of interiors and wallpapers and the business name, Manolo Walls. She also had commented that this business name had come to her while at a Christian concert. I immediately knew what artist and song she was referring to, and I messaged her and struck up a conversation. Her reply was so kind and friendly that it caused me to look further onto her site, and I saw her store's location was in Portland, Oregon. Lightbulb moment! I got excited, and my logic was still, "Maybe I can photograph her shop and feature her company on my blog!" I proposed the idea of a collaboration, and she agreed and told me to reach back out when my arrival date was closer.

About two weeks before leaving for Oregon, I went to message her, and I found myself stuck yet again. I didn't really know what to propose. Sure a quick pop in her shop might be fun, but what could I pitch to her that would also benefit her business? I stopped before acting and let it just rest for a moment. And I prayed. Therein lied the power, and I heard the words deep within the recesses of my heart, "The Marriage Project." The questions started popping into my mind, "Is she married?" I checked her account. Yes, she was. "Would they be open to talking about a very intimate, vulnerable subject with a complete stranger?" I wasn't so sure. I decided to step out in faith and go for it. I paused before writing out my vision for this and took a deep breath wanting to convey the message just right. This is what I wrote:

> I was going to reach out a couple days ago but waited a couple more to see if any fresh ideas came to mind about what we talked about a few weeks ago regarding a shoot. And I'm so glad I waited because as I was in the Word this morning and praying, I feel led to share with you something that the Lord has been putting on my heart for some time now. As a wedding photographer, I feel this calling to shine a light on the sanctity of marriage and to begin a project sharing couples' stories and testimonies behind Christ-centered marriages. It's been a little over a year since the idea first sprang up in my mind, and I've felt Him highlight certain couples to interview with photos to accompany it as well.

So that new idea is that! Just wanted to see if you and your husband would even (a) both be available one of the 5 days I'll be in Portland and (b) willing to do a marriage shoot / record a little interview?

I hit send. And then immediately got down on the floor and prayed. It's always a super humbling experience putting your heart on the line, and that's exactly what that message felt like. I couldn't imagine the emotion of ever being proposed to and saying "yes" and the vulnerability in that season and the shakiness of nerves and excitement on a wedding day. I was thankful I had plenty of time to build up for when that moment comes. I wanted all of what I sent to be received the way it was intended to be and really was just praying the fear of rejection out of me. This was the first time I'd really shared this idea with anyone I didn't know, and I was nervous that the response would be something like the responses I'd grown used to hearing, "no." But then I remembered none of this was about me or my insecurities. The moment had come to step into boldness and bravery, and the worst that could happen were more crickets. It's always more freeing to do the scary thing and face it square on, no matter the outcome.

I decided to get out of the house and ended up with a friend who went with me for a walk. I was recounting to her all the back-story, and she told me to check my messages to see whether I'd gotten a response yet. I'd gotten used to all the "no" replies or zero responses, so quite honestly, I was bracing myself for the same. I can imagine, God was just giddy to prove me wrong. This was finally the striking of gold, the striking of His heart and His intended purpose for my summer and calling, the one I'd been waiting to discover since Haiti. I love how He works because when there's been mul-tiple rejections, when the "yes" comes it bolsters our confidence that this is absolutely His will because He shut all those other doors knowing this is the one He had been waiting to open.

The response I received had me grinning ear to ear, and the message had me in awe. Not only did she reply quickly, she replied above and beyond what I could have hoped for. God's fingerprints were all over it. She said she would be in town that weekend and that she and her husband would love to be a part of this project. She shared they loved the heart and mission of it and that she also knew two other couples who had powerful stories of breakthrough in their marriages, and they'd be more than willing to talk and interview with me as well. Excitement and emotions were at an all-time high.

In all honesty, unbelief set in almost immediately. I was still a bit unsure if this would actually happen. Schedules change last minute, these other couples had children, so I held onto the promise lightly but with great hope for what God had in store for that weekend in Portland. And this verse was directed right at my small faith: "You of little faith, why are you so afraid?" (Matt. 8:26). Why was I always so afraid? God was about to rock my socks off.

The First Testimony

I exchanged phone numbers with the women who'd be participating and we made plans and set times to meet up with each couple once my friend and I landed in Portland. We had a very small window of time to fit in a photo shoot and interview with three couples with a wedding to attend right in the middle of it all. With Jesus in charge of all the details, there was a perfect time and day that worked for all of us. Nelli and Art (couple #1) would meet us Friday at Crystal Springs Rhododendron Garden, picnic basket packed and all. Nelli also insisted that any sort of "thank you" for what they were doing was not necessary because they were doing this for the same reason I was. Their heart was to glorify the Lord through their marriage and testimony, no other reason than that.

As Friday afternoon came, my friend and I sat in the car in the parking lot, and I started to feel overwhelmed. I wanted to do a job well done, and I knew how long photo shoots could take. But in that moment, I heard the Lord speak, "It's not about the photos." It was more about the stories, the hearts, and the testimonies. The initial meet up with Nelli and Art was completely natural, and as we first met, we got to sharing about our lives and began strolling around the park looking for some photo spots. Without the pressure of spending too much time on the photos, we moved quickly through taking pictures and set the picnic blanket in a quiet spot in the park and went right into the interview. I shared with them that this was my first time ever doing this and that they were my guinea pigs. They were very gracious and were ready for whatever happened—even when that meant hitting pause on the recording app on my phone to avoid a family of raccoons creeping in on our space. And that's right, I said phone. I didn't have a mic yet, just my phone and a heart desiring to glorify God. Let that be an encouragement to just start with what you have, and God will do the rest.

After about two hours spent at the park, Nelli and Art were ready to caravan with my friend and I to meet with their friends in Washougal, Washington, for the next interview and photo session. Rick and Michele (couple #2) have three young boys and needed a babysitter to make this work. Nelli and Art gave up their Friday night to free Rick and Michele up to do the interview and photo shoot—total Godsends.

We all made the drive up and over the Columbia River to cross over into Washington. The GPS guided us through beautiful country back roads, with rays of sunlight lighting up the tall tips of grass (like my vision at the start of this all, walking with Jesus in my white dress). We lost service as we made our way down the last turn, pulling up to a tree-lined road as we reached our destination. Rick and the two oldest boys came out to greet us and welcome us in. Nelli and Art were right behind us. We walked into their home, and Michele embraced us as if we'd known her for years. Rick shared a really cool story about their house, that it had once been a barn. Rick had taken on his own project and completely gutted and renovated this once barn and made it into a home for his family.

The greater story was during the building of their house, one of the workers who had helped reconstruct the barn had an encounter with the Holy Spirit there. Rick had shared the gospel with this man, and the man believed and wanted to give his life to Christ. As he laid the tile, he made a cross with it, and on the concrete below the tile he wrote, "The house where I was saved." Hearing this, I knew where we stood was holy ground. What was about to be spoken was anointed. This home was a home that served the Lord, and everything about that night solidified to me God's heart for marriage and the family.

That entire afternoon and evening was glorious. We drove home late because between the photos and stopping for some dinner, we didn't conclude Rick and Michele's interview portion until well after midnight. We stayed up laughing. Michele made us London Fogs, and they sent us out, praying over my friend and I and *our* future marriages. I was relishing in all God was doing...and the late sunsets—we're talking 8:30–9:00 p.m. in Oregon during summertime. My heart was full to the brim. How could it possibly hold more? We still had one more couple to meet that Monday, and as Monday afternoon came, I couldn't even imagine what was in store. As we drove down the freeway, taking in all the greenery, we passed a sign that said, "Portland: City of Roses." I couldn't help but smile at the precious hand of God and feel Him romancing my heart once more. I realized roses were one of the traces of His wooing love in my life, even before I discovered Him as First Love.

The Love Flower

I remembered the rose bush at the very most corner of my house growing up. The petals of the roses were a blush pink and always bloomed come springtime. My mom would cut a few of them off the vine and bring them inside, filling the house with their aroma. She would fill a glass vase with water from the garden hose and arrange the stems in such a way that each rose would be seen, setting some higher than another. I hadn't thought about those roses in quite some time. But as I thought about this flower and saw that sign in Portland, I began to sense a pattern—a trail of rose petals that had been left throughout my entire life, left by God. Through some of the narrowest and most treacherous paths in my life, there were traces of them. Roses were symbolic of God's love pursuing me all of my days. One thing I know to be true about roses is that they require seasonal pruning. Like our hearts. According to *Better Homes and Gardens*, it's important to prune roses because "pruning removes diseased and dead stems and canes and reduces the overall size of the plant. The first spring bloom demonstrates how pruning results in an annual process of renewal."

An annual process of renewal. Annual meaning once every year, so I could expect to go through some sort of cut back, removal of diseased, dead parts every year? *Okay, Lord.*

"Renewal" is a word I like especially when its meaning is having to do with repairing something that's broken, worn out, or run down. Doesn't it seem we need some pruning and renewal on the daily? All of that pruning and renewing, helping us get closer to reaching those small goals we set for ourselves. Along with "annual," another word I'd become closely acquainted with was "process." The process can get grueling, and it definitely requires a lot of patience to be worked in. The definition of the word "process" is "a series of actions or steps taken in order to achieve a particular end." If it were left up to me, I'd have little to no growth because I'm impatient by nature. But with God as the Pruner of our hearts, we're well on our way to becoming more and more like His Son, Jesus, who is astoundingly patient.

Thankfully, He *never* tires or never stops working. John 5:17 states, "Jesus said to them, 'My Father is always at his work to this very day, and I too am working.'" That brings such relief to my heart and I can rest assured that even when I feel like I'm not making progress or the process is feeling really tedious, God is at work on my behalf.

What has since stood out to me is Jesus's crown being described as a crown of thorns and how that ties into this trace of roses. I was reading through Mark one day and chapter 15, verse 17 reads, "They dressed him in a purple robe, and they wove thorn branches into a crown and put it on his head." I'd read this verse many times, but this time, the words that jumped off the page were, "a crown of long, sharp thorns..." My first thought was, "Where in the world did these Roman soldiers come up with this crown?" So I dug a little deeper. The first symbolism of thorns dates back to when Adam and Eve sinned, bringing a curse upon the world. Genesis 3:17–18 states, "Cursed is the ground because of you; in pain you shall eat of it all the days of your life; thorns and thistles it shall bring forth for you..."

How pleasant are thorns and thistles? Not very. It's the stuff you have to avoid on your hikes. Those little spiky thorns and bristles that get stuck in your socks hurt! Because of sin entering the world, this is the ramification—weeds, thistles, thorns—pain, suffering, sorrow. I began looking more into the meaning behind thorns and thistles in the Bible. I found a lot of information. In an online article I came upon this, "Thorns and thistles throughout the Bible remind us of the historical Original Sin and Curse that followed. The negative biblical overtones associated with thorns and thistles after Genesis 3:18 are demonstrated in their representation as obstacles, punishment, or serving as a reminder of sin and its consequences." This same article includes these Scripture references: Numbers 33:55, Proverbs 15:19, Isaiah 34:13, Matthew 13:3–8, and Hebrews 6:8, with the ultimate fulfillment of the symbolism that thorns and thistles have in the Bible is found in Matthew 27:29.

I went back to read from the gospel of Matthew, with a similar retelling of Jesus's trial and how he was treated by the soldiers. "Some of the governor's soldiers took Jesus into their headquarters and called out the entire regiment. They stripped him and put a scarlet robe on him. They wove thorn branches into a crown and put it on his head..." (Matt. 27:27–29, NLT). This is the ultimate fulfillment of the symbolism of the thorns and thistles, Jesus's crown of thorns. In Matthew 27:29 we have the Roman soldiers unknowingly (yet not coincidentally) weaving Jesus a crown made out of thorns. They took an object of the curse and fashioned it into a crown for the One who was about to deliver us from that very curse. Here's the Amplified Bible version:

> And after twisting together a crown of thorns, they put it on His head, and put a reed in His right hand [as a scepter]. Kneeling before Him, they ridiculed Him, saying, "Hail, King of the Jews!" (Matt. 27:29).

The depiction we so often see of Jesus if we look to art or Google is a bloodied man, on a cross with a crown of *dead*, thorny brambles upon His head. There are many theories as to the type of thorns these were. I'd like to add my unofficial theory into the running. The word "wove," or "weave," caught my attention. In the New Living Translation version of Matthew 27:29 that is the word that is used. And my thoughts went to, "How could someone weave any sort of dead branch?" To weave means to interlace, twist, or braid. So where did this idea come from that they were *dead* branches? And for argument's sake, if they were in fact dead and dry to create a circular shape such as a crown wouldn't they snap and break? My theory is that this crown of thorns wasn't dead at all. I imagine it to be alive and green. A woven braid of multiple stems. But what type of flower or bush has thorny stems? A rose bush. The courts Jesus was taken through could arguably have had rose bushes around and perhaps between the many hours that passed between them making this crown and the ascent to the hill where Jesus took up the cross, the thorns had withered and browned. But before sounding naive and leading from the whimsical place in my mind, I researched rose bushes in Judea and Jerusalem, and it would seem that at the time Jesus was alive perhaps this was one of the only flowers approved to grow per an article I read online about Jerusalem's roses.

"There was a time in Jerusalem when, with the notable exception of roses, cultivation of plants was forbidden. 2000 years ago, when the Holy Temple still stood within Jerusalem's walls, no gardens could be planted because of the smells of rot and decay associated with decomposing vegetation and manure that well-tended gardens may produce. Unpleasant odors could not be allowed in the vicinity of God's sanctuary. For two reasons, growing roses in Jerusalem was permitted, despite the overall ban on horticultural activity in the capital city. The first was tradition. To quote from the Talmud (Babylonian Talmud,

Bava Kama, 82b), there had been rose gardens in Jerusalem "from the days of the first prophets." The other reason rose gardens were permitted in Jerusalem was that, according to Rashi, the Medieval commentator, roses were used as an additive to the Temple incense mixture, which was burned twice a day."

While I know Jesus wasn't near the Temple on the day of His crucifixion, I found it interesting that it said in all of Jerusalem the cultivation of plants was forbidden, all expect for the rose. The Israeli rose does look quite a bit different than the roses we associate with a rose, but nonetheless it intrigued me. Whether this can be proven or not, I can't help but think would it not be like God who sent His Son to die for us to demonstrate His love for us with the very same thorny flower that we still use to this day to say, "I love you"? I believe He could have sent this message through any crown of thorns, but I like this idea. And this would be the furthest tracing back to the trail of rose petals He's left me—and left you, tracing all the way back to the cross.

I wanted to include this to invite you to look back on your life. Do you see the rose petals traced throughout your life? They may not be literal rose petals, but do you remember a time the Lord spoke in the darkest places of your life? Did you hear a whisper and ignore it? I think on all the ways He's shown Himself to me, from that first rosebush, to my three rose tattoos (all which I got before walking with God), to my first friend in the faith who had a rose garden in the front of her house, to Portland, Oregon, and opening up an adventure called The Marriage Project in the City of Roses. Jesus wants us to see Him, and He wants to be in relationship with us. His love isn't based on the gamble of plucking off rose petals and landing on the "He loves me" of the "He loves me, loves me not" game. It's settled, He loves you.

I See A Rose in Bloom

As I walked around the Rose Garden in Washington Park during some of our free time, I was enamored. The experience was all so fresh and vibrant the week after, but as time passes, we sometimes forget all the Lord has done in our lives, and more of the process takes place. It's important to remember the pivotal moments in our journey with God. If there's something coming to mind now as you read these words, stop, remember, write it down. Ask the Holy Spirit to reignite that flame that was once there that has since been extinguished or needs rekindling. Perhaps it's a dream or a promise God had given you. Maybe you've let the opinion of others shape who you've become, and you don't even recognize yourself anymore. The voice of an abusive person in your life has made you devalue yourself and given you a cynical perspective. The loud world, social media, music, or countless other things have drowned out the voice you know is Truth. Ask God to remove the disease that's covering the bud below. This is a bud that He wants to nurture and prune so that growth can happen. You can be that rose in bloom that just needs the loving Gardener's touch to have fragrance and beauty spring forth once more.

"They triumphed over him by the blood of the Lamb and by the word of their testimony; they did not love their lives so much as to shrink from death."

— Revelation 12:11

9

A Strand of Three Cords

"And if one can overpower him who is alone, two can resist him.
A cord of three *strands* is not quickly torn apart."
— Ecclesiastes 4:12

T his is where it gets good. This is the meat of what the project is all about! I'm so happy you're still here, still with me. I hope to do a spinoff book with more of the testimonies I've collected along the journey. Since you've made it this far, I wanted to give you an exclusive first look of what that book would hold. But really, I share it because the testimony of my story and the testament of this project aren't quite complete without sharing all that I heard from the other two Oregon couples God led me to interview too. Both have powerful testimonies.

My hope in sharing these are twofold: (1) that you might see the way God works through a surrendered and open heart as you wait for the right person to come in His right timing if you are desiring a relationship, and (2) for you to see the blessing it is to wait for God's handpicked person for you. Waiting for God's best doesn't guarantee that marriage will be pure bliss the entirety of your relationship, but rather, it will be more desirous knowing you let God pick the person He knows complements you best. Persisting on in a toxic, unhealthy relationship with someone who doesn't share your same values can result in years of heartache and unnecessary hardship. Rick and Michele's story proves that nothing can stand in the way of God's plan for the relationship He has prepared or is preparing you for. It doesn't matter what your past looks like. God redeems broken people, broken hearts, broken marriages—He does it all.

It is powerful having the Holy Spirit intercede on behalf of a marriage, and it's evident how much God loves marriage and how fighting for a marriage is worth it. Fighting for purity before marriage will be worth it for your future marriage, and fighting for a broken marriage will be worth it for your future family and future generations.

On this journey, I've discovered why God designed marriage the way He did. It not only demonstrates His covenant love but was established (1) to be a symbol of loyalty between a husband and wife, (2) as a tool to learn how to receive and offer forgiveness (a portrait of God's forgiveness), (3) as the firmest foundation for a family with His command to "be fruitful and multiply" (Gen. 1:28) and to train them in the way of the Lord (Deut. 6:6–7, Jl. 1:3, Ps. 78:4), and (4) to build an intimacy like no other relationship has (read the Song of Songs book of the Bible to see what I mean).

So here is a part of Rick and Michele Andersen's testimonies with Mitch and Maria Vorobets' marriage testimony in the next chapter.

Handpicked Gifts

Rick Andersen was born in Denver, Colorado. Michele was raised in Palm Springs, California, in a Christian home. Rick was raised in a Catholic, Latino home. His mom passed away when he was 7 years old, and it sent the family reeling. Rick shares, "Life went from really amazing to really dark. My stepmom wasn't God-fearing at all. She basically told me, 'We come from monkeys.'" He accepted that, didn't ask any further questions, and with that new perspective Rick began adapting to animal-like behavior.

Rick describes his life from a young child to about 27 as trying to do his best, always wanting to be the center of attention, and always trying to bring people together, yet he felt it never worked. Then he fell in love with a girl. He says, "I became angry and was completely shattered after that 7-year relationship ended. It crashed very ugly due to a drug addiction. I made myself to become someone else over the next three years. I was pretty much leading Satan's parade, growing marijuana, listening to heavy metal."

"At age 29, Jesus showed up and said, 'You're looking for truth? I'm it.' He radically, radically saved me while I was trying to prove Him wrong. He had called me to forgive a friend who had deceived me. He had stolen from me." That must have been hard, and Rick had said it was a test. "Unknowingly, this friend was about to end his life. As I was on my way to forgive him, God showed me my life in his life. That's when the power of God came upon me for the first time, and I preached the gospel to him. All the hate fell off of me and love, and peace and joy came into my life in that moment. It had been a three-month process to have me seal the deal in making a covenant with God." But at that moment he was all in, received Christ, and through that process, not only had he been saved but helped save a friend.

Rick then felt God call him to attend Bible college in Spain. Before leaving, a very conservative couple spoke a prophetic word to him (which was a bit out of place coming from them). They encouraged him by saying, "Don't care what anybody is going to say, especially your family. Just go...oh, and by the way, your wife is at Bible college." Rick wasn't seeking marriage, but this was what was spoken to him. He also heard another truth bomb, this time it was that still, small voice of the Lord's...*"If you go seeking Me, I'll reveal her to you."* Rick wasn't so sure, but one thing he was sure of was he was going to Spain.

Michele popped in the interview at this point with her cute little voice saying, "That's me!" in reference to who Jesus would reveal to Rick as his wife. But there were still a lot of things to work out first.

Upon arriving in Spain, Rick says, "I see this girl at Bible college coming in, smokin' from the world. She had a 50 lb. suitcase filled with clubbing and beach clothes, these were very small pieces of material and very high shoes..." Michele chimes in, "Party island. Mom and dad thought Bible college, I was thinking something entirely different."

Rick noticed Michele but had been used to communication that wasn't honoring to women, so he thought, "No way am I ever going near this girl. Especially this 19-year old girl..." Michele chimes in again, "I like a challenge" and laughed. She thought Rick was cute and wanted to talk to him. She shares, "The 50 lb. suitcase of clothes was super humbling once I got there, and I had to explain myself. My parents have always loved the Lord, they both come from rough backgrounds. I've had a lot of overseas missions experience with them. I had a sense of entitlement because if my parents love Jesus that must mean I love Jesus, right? I always stood back in awe that they gave their life for others, but I hadn't ever had experienced it myself."

Even knowing all she had been taught and all she had observed doing missions work, she still had that rebel heart rise up. Her parents finally gave her an ultimatum. She was to go to Bible college, or she was no longer welcome in their house. She agreed to Bible college, but that's where she was secretly thinking she'd make the experience "party island." The air of entitlement preceded her, and she went in thinking she was going to grace everybody with her presence, she wanted to pop their little bubble—all these virgins or pastor's daughters. Yet the Lord had another idea. She was surprised as she had an entirely different perspective walking in. Michele shares they transformed right before her eyes, they weren't uppity prudes but beautiful daughters of the Lord. God began to show her what true beauty was through these girls. They extended so much grace and never reprimanded her for what she was wearing. She suddenly saw that they were set apart, and she got to see in a really pure way what it meant to be holy.

Satan started to attack her thoughts, and she felt like the black sheep, like she didn't belong. She started to feel isolated, and a lot of shame and condemnation came over her. That's when Rick decided it was time he stepped in. He was this older guy who she says she was definitely attracted to and he deliberately didn't share his testimony with her because that was an intimate thing, and while he wanted to encourage her, he didn't want to get involved any further than that.

She knew he could relate to her (that he had a past too), and he could see the heaviness of the shame she was carrying. Instead of succumbing to that feeling, he encouraged her to press in to all God had for her there; otherwise, she was going to miss out. She couldn't help but be attracted to the healthy communication that they kept going, yet Rick defined the relationship early on to clarify there were boundaries, and this was no more than a friendship. Defining the relationship is so important in a guy-girl relationship as it can eliminate so much confusion and unintentional or unwanted intimacy.

As Michele's time at Bible college continued, she was seeing the Lord as the Potter, and she was the clay (Isa. 64:8) and He was breaking down all the idols in her life, similar to what He had done in my life. She says at this point she was excited to be experiencing God in a personal way and for the first time genuinely wanted to go on this adventure with Him. She says, "Now that I had stepped out of my bubble and into reality, there was this messy trail I left behind me, and I asked, 'What are you going to do with this, Lord?'"

Michele shares that while she was beginning to fall in love with the Lord, she was also falling in love with someone else, Rick. She was seeing him serving others, seeing his heart for worship, his personal hunger for the Lord, and his prayer in a group setting was so intimate, praying "the closet prayers" in front of everyone, and it was all so sincere and genuine, and she desired that.

She made the decision to be baptized, which is simply an outward reflection of being born again and of the inner heart change taking place. Rick said through that action he saw a real choice for God from Michele, and he had a brief thought of breaking his own friendship rule with her. But he shares his thoughts were, "Don't mess this up now by trying to make a romance out of this. Don't put a bunch of weight on the girl."

He says all the relationships he tried both in Christianity and outside had been shipwrecks and resulted in ruined friendships. He was sure he still didn't want to be in a relationship at all. However, there were feelings that had developed for Michele that had to be addressed.

He asked if they could talk the last week of school, and she agreed. Rick was direct. He said, "You're going to make a great wife for someone one day but you're 19. You're 19, and you just had an island experience. You need to face some real life first. Me? I don't plan on kissing anyone else until marriage. I'm not wasting any more time." I failed to mention there was a significant age difference between the two of them. Which was another contributing reason to him being very cautious in moving forward in any sort of romantic relationship. What happened next was the only thing

Michele could have said that would have thrown Rick for an absolute loop. She humbled herself in that moment and said she'd seen his heart over the last couple of months and had fallen in love with his heart. Rick said, "She didn't understand the depth of what she just said." He was pretty shaken and wasn't sure how to proceed forward, so he went to one of the pastor's houses to ask for wisdom and for accountability.

Then there was the divine intervention. As they had been talking, they had been walking together near a road that had been closed down much of their time in Spain. They weren't expecting any oncoming traffic as they hadn't ever seen any cars on that particular road. Yet all of a sudden, they heard a car coming, and it was coming fast.

Michele lost her balance and had somehow fallen down right in front of the fast approaching car. Rick says the Spirit or an angel had him throw his arm out to pull her back. As he did so, her foot came out of its joint, she says she remember it felt like her foot was ripped off. If Rick hadn't acted so quickly the car would have hit her. The car zoomed passed as Rick sat her down. As he knelt to help her, he realized this was the first time they had had any physical contact, and as it happened, he says he heard the word "home."

Michele shares that as the reality of what had just happened started to set in, she began feeling shooting pain, but another thought came to mind too. She laughs, "I just got my foot ran over by a car, and in the midst of all of it I thought, 'This feels really nice.'" She was referring to Rick's arms around her. Rick got Michele to the hospital, and the pastor that Rick had gone to for accountability met both of them at the hospital. The pastor went up to Rick and said, "It's great that you're here right now...but only if you want to marry Michele. If you don't want to marry her, then you need to leave." It was clear that to continue to invest in this woman would need a solid commitment, it was that serious to protect her heart. The pastor could see the affect Rick had on Michele, and it needn't progress any further if Rick had no intention in being more deeply committed to Michele at some point in his life. Rick says he took that seriously, went outside to pray, and as he did so, this supernatural peace came over him. He thought that "if she'd have me, she'll be my wife." God started awakening him to a love for her, and another sobering thought came to mind, "What if she had passed away?" and he started weeping. As closed off as he'd been to relationships, God was doing a work in his heart. In that moment, Rick says, "I saw her dancing around my heart bringing it back to life. She's been everything I ever needed and nothing I ever expected" Rick says.

It was a harrowing but miraculous way to bring these two sinners once afar off to know God as First Love first and then to awaken them to love and to each other. They shared that since being married they have been through very difficult trials in their marriage but have also seen the miraculous many times over. Michele was told her foot would never heal right and that she'd be lame the rest of her life, but God! When I met her, she was walking on both feet and had been fully healed. Their second son was born 95% deaf, told he would live this way his entire life, yet through fasting and praying for him, when they reran tests, everything was cleared. This isn't to say God has to work in these ways to be worthy of praise. It's more a matter of our heart posture in the midst of our suffering and hardest moments, knowing He is good no matter what He brings us to and through in this life. Every suffering, every pain will one day be gone, and it's what we hope for and what we're promised to experience in eternity with Him.

Celebrating 13 Years

Ten years into their marriage (at the time of the interview) they share they were just finally starting to be in sync with one another. Rick says, "You say yes to a covenant, but what you're really saying yes to is a future event, one that you're going to spend learning to walk into. Michele and I are so different. Our strengths are totally polar opposites, but we have learned patience through it, letting Him show us how He sees us." In both, the good and the bad, marriage is a humbling thing. They are celebrating thirteen years of marriage this year.

I asked them what marriage is or to define it as best they know how. Rick said, "Marriage is a covenant, not a contract. It is a choice to come into a relationship with someone else where heaven meets earth like no other. You want to look at the trinity (Father, Son, Holy Spirit—God being three in one) and want to see a resemblance of what that is? Look no further than marriage. I feel sorry for people that take marriage lightly. If you don't have Jesus as the third chord strand, you are entering in without a real connection. When Jesus is at the core of it, and your flesh and your strength fail you, the truth prevails. The truth is not of this realm."

Michele shares, "Marriage has been such an honor and a gift from the Lord." She shared when she was growing up and imagined her husband, that Rick is better than she could have imagined. "He's a handpicked gift, and I look at our children and I think God has given so much. We have this opportunity to represent Christ in our marriage in a real way, in a genuine way. So many see marriages that are awful, and children do not have a safe place, and we get to break any past patterns and create something new and pure for our children that is Christ centered. You don't have to be married to feel complete because He fills that." Michele does share she feels so complete as a wife and mom, and she's living one of her dreams. She didn't know what it would look like, but it's better than she imagined.

Rick honestly shares this too, "I never wanted to be married. It seemed painful and hard, and I was too self-centered. I couldn't imagine being with one woman. Yet God gave me His heart, and when we got married our wedding day was the first time we kissed on the lips..." "Which was crazy for both of us knowing both of our pasts," Michele chimes in. Rick continues, "We had both poured our fountains out in the streets (Prov. 5:16), but I can tell you straighter than straight, I have never had any other experience like our marriage bed, which is something undefiled. God's blessing is on our relationship. There's no looking over my shoulder, no negative because of that...it's all 'Yes and amen.' And as we learned to trust each other and Him with the sanctity of our marriage and everything we do to show heaven on earth in our relationship, it has been blessed by him, and it is holy. As we learn to enjoy each other in every aspect of how He made us, we are not to be ashamed, and we enter into the garden."

They also keep it real and shared, "Don't get me wrong, it's hard. If you see a marriage where there's nothing wrong, something is wrong because somewhere life has to be real, but the reward of Jesus in the center is unlike any drug I've ever had, unlike any mountaintop experience, unlike any jumping out of an airplane. There's no comparison to having God at the center of a marriage, and not just saying it but living it."

10

A Marriage Redeemed

"And I said to God, 'God, I don't love him, I don't trust him.'
And I heard Him say back, 'Don't love him, don't trust him.
Love Me, trust Me.'"
—Maria Vorobets

M itch and Maria were the third couple I met up with while
in Portland, Oregon, in July of 2017. I met them on the last
evening we were there. My friend and I pulled up to their house;
they had two babysitters ready to watch their four kids and hopped
in our rental car. I thought, "Who are these people?" They were so
great to believe the vision of this project so much to not only get
sitters but to hop in the car with perfect strangers to go take some
photos and tell me about their marriage story.

However, that's a testimony in and of itself to how tightly knit
the family of God is. We are united in cause and in Christ, and it's
truly amazing how interwoven our stories are because we are part
of a larger story. His story.

One of the first things Maria said after we exchanged introduc-
tions was, "I know this amazing spot. It's about an hour away though;
is that okay?" Of course it was! We recorded on my phone, in the car
on the way to this most amazing spot, Rowena Crest. Maria is also

a wedding photographer—we had that in common. And when we arrived, the location was stunning. Its view did not disappoint.

Mitch and Maria

Maria and her family are from Ukraine. Mitch and his family are from Romania. Maria grew up in a Christian home. Mitch visited the church she was going to, a Slavic church, in Portland, and he said, "It was love at first sight."

Mitch was 20, almost 21, and Maria was 15. They got to know each other very slowly as their parents were against them dating. Mitch started pursuing Maria, picking her up for youth events, and the relationship started there. Despite Maria's mom sitting them down and putting rules around their dating, a week later Maria came home with a ring on her finger. Mitch was a great guy, so they did bless the engagement. They share they took their engagement slow until legal age. Maria grew up with little to no communication with her parents and didn't know what to expect before marriage, and Mitch and Maria did not have any premarital counseling. "I didn't know how God intended marriage to be, I'd never even heard it preached or had had a solid example to look up to," Maria shares.

They both admit to having filters on going into marriage. Four months in to their marriage, they started hitting potholes. Maria shares intimacy and sex were difficult that first year because of a traumatic thing she had gone through as a child and because she hadn't learned to communicate or the importance of communication, she shut Mitch out.

Instead of sharing with Mitch why she was recoiling from intimacy and sex, Maria kept her distance but thought or hoped he would understand without sharing her feelings. Yet he shares he felt rejected in the moment.

What they weren't getting at home, they allowed themselves to look for from the outside world, which opened up a new can of worms. They admit they dealt with their problems unhealthily. Maria and Mitch did get pregnant, yet the pregnancies were awful—Maria says there was a lot of bed rest, morning sickness all 9 months, and it was even more difficult on their new marriage. Yet Maria says Mitch was very supportive, trying to help, but again, communication was lacking.

Maria says, "Because we didn't know how to communicate, we were building our own assumptions on what was going on." From Mitch's point of view, he was not understanding his new wife and began believing lies—thinking, "Is she hiding something?" They did have good moments, but they were dealing with the problems in their own strength when they should have brought them to the Lord and talked about them together but didn't. They just kept living life to themselves. Mitch emphasizes this by saying it felt like they were living two separate lives, enjoying home when at home together, but then also living lives away from each other.

Maria said, "I had ladies night out, the guys would get together, that's how we did life. That was our normal. As much as I'd like to say we had Christ in the middle, I don't believe He was there. We didn't invite Him into our marriage—we thought we could do it on our own."

Fast-forward, four kids later, two separate lives, being jealous of each other, life felt quiet, but the shoe was about to drop—and the breaking point did come, after their fourth child. Because they were not focused on the same things, as a husband and wife, Maria shares she became emotionally attached to another man she met. In the midst of this, there had been other things happening in their close to 10 years of marriage. She felt Mitch wasn't giving her enough. Mitch also admitted to infidelities on his part as he plunged further into those feelings of rejection from his wife. Maria had begun to give up on her marriage and didn't want to try anymore at all. It didn't seem as if there was a reason to, especially since she had let this other man in. At that point, she knew it was too far gone. The arguing got worse, both were very defensive, they were completely against each other.

Finally Mitch reached his breaking point and told her everything: how he'd been dealing with stuff, how he'd been feeling from day one, and she reciprocated. A whole decade of garbage spilled out onto each other. They share they felt like they had nothing to lose because it felt like it was over. Everything was out on the table. There was no way this marriage would sustain, and ash was blowing everywhere, a marriage disintegrated. They decided they were going to get a divorce. However, Mitch shares that he still had some kind of peace, like everything was going to be okay.

Mitch says, "I couldn't believe that was the end, even though it was. It was hard to picture a future, but it was harder to picture a future without Maria and the kids." This realization made him really set out on a journey of seeking the Lord. Maria shares in the midst of the most hurtful parts, the most broken parts in that moment felt like she was the closest to God, and she started crying out to Him. As she began talking to God, she shares a bit of what she spoke out loud to God, "Obviously, we can't do this at all. In our own strengths we can't make anything work, we can't even sit in a room and talk like civilized people. But okay...God if you want this marriage to exist, if you brought us two together for a reason, or whatever this is, whatever is left of it, You have to make the marriage be what it was intended for."

That was a Sunday night. In the early morning hours, around 4 a.m., Maria's mom came into her room as she and the kids had gone to stay with her parents for a few nights.

"My mom and dad wanted to talk to me. They knew my side of the story, but Mitch went to them. He cried and apologized at how he'd been treating me, what he'd been going through and wanted prayer and support. I defended myself and stated biblical grounds for divorce, infidelities had happened on both sides...my heart was done. But my dad said, 'Technically you have the right to do that but only if he is still living in that sin and choosing not to repent. But when this man is seeking God with his whole heart for his family and for your marriage, you do not have that right.'" That hit her hard. She reluctantly let Mitch move back in the house even though she says her heart remained hard and doubtful.

Maria didn't want to believe he was a changed man. She was skeptical and didn't want to do this all over again. She thought it would be easier to let go and start over. She says, "So I just sat back in the living room, didn't want to make eye contact with Mitch, and I just let him be in the home, but all of a sudden I started seeing him through different eyes. The moment I gave it all to God, He let me see him how He saw him. It was so beautiful. He was so different. Mitch was more intentional, spoke to the kids differently, at one point he was washing the dishes, and I said to him, 'You don't have to do this. This is ridiculous, put the dishes down...' and all he said in return was, 'Just let me love you.' And I said to God, 'God, I don't love him, I don't trust him.' And I heard Him say back, 'Don't love him, don't trust him. Love Me, trust Me.' So I backed off and let God do his thing and let Mitch do his. He really loved on the kids, loved on the home, woke up really early, spending time with the Lord, these new things were happening. It gave life, it was fresh. This was a new beginning. It was very fragile, I didn't know how to be in the same room. He didn't know if he could put his arm around me, it was very... just fragile."

Breakthrough

Around that time, some of their friends invited them to church. They hadn't been in church in such a long time. They accepted the invite and went to a Friday night service. They had never been a part of a setting where the focus of the night was letting the Spirit move, they were not brought up in that culture. Mitch asked Maria, "Are you uncomfortable?" And whether she was or not, she said she couldn't move but just started crying.

A teenager walked up to them and said, "Hey, I don't know if this makes any sense to you, but during worship I saw the word 'breakthrough' over your heads." More tears. That was confirmation that God saw them and that He was answering that prayer of Maria's heart. From that point on they just sat back and watched Him work in their lives and marriage. Maria says, "If you've watched Cinderella and know the scene when the fairy Godmother waves her wand over Cinderella's dress and it goes from rags to a sparkling ball gown, that was our marriage. I heard God say, 'I love you, and I love your marriage.'"

Three years after that, they renewed their vows. They share the last four years have been absolutely beautiful and share how God redeemed their marriage. They recently welcomed a fifth baby girl! Maria says, "He's done so much, I'm always in awe. And we're just enjoying partnering with God and having Him be at the center of our marriage now. When we have disagreements, our kids will tell us to go pray about it. Our priority is no longer ourselves but is each other."

I asked them "What is marriage?" Maria answered, "Marriage is Christ and the church. What He's done, what Jesus did and paid the price for His church. We're flawed, we're human, yet He saw so much worth in us and called us by name. He didn't call our flaws out but called the gold out. Mitch chooses to see past my flaws and loves me in spite of them. And I do the same...I try to. It's a work in progress...I know God...He's so infinite and there's so much mystery to Him, and forever and ever we will be discovering His heart. There are layers upon layers to discover, and I feel the same about marriage and my husband. When I am 90, I will still be discovering sweet things and new layers of Mitch I hadn't known when I was 30. This is an adventure we're going on and I'm just excited."

Mitch shared, "If you go all the way back to why we had our problems, we didn't go into understanding what marriage is. That is the biggest mistake, and people still make it. We try to put our best selves out there and hide other things we don't want the other person to know. And that creates a foundation based on a lie. It leaves too much room for the enemy to attack. In my case, I wish I knew a lot of the stuff she went through as a child, that was the reason certain things didn't happen the way I thought it should or expected it to from the start, and that created so many problems. If I would have known, I would have loved to be right there next to her and help her through it, but for the sake of putting our best selves forward, that didn't happen.

We just need to be there for each other and help each other. I like when she messes up because I can be there and help her with that. That's what marriage is, helping each other and thinking for the other first.

Until we realized we're not perfect, but we actually love each other being imperfect, and that we're together to improve, you know, together, hand in hand, that's the goal of marriage."

"'For your Creator will be your husband; the LORD of Heaven's Armies is his name! He is your Redeemer, the Holy One of Israel, the God of all the Earth. For the LORD has called you back from your grief— as though you were a young wife abandoned by her husband,' says your God."

— Isaiah 54:5–6

11

Marriage, Divorce, the Altar and Adam and Eve

"Most important of all, continue to show deep love for each other,
for love covers a multitude of sins."
— 1 Peter 4:8

I t's 2021 and the war declared against what marriage is and who defines it is at an all-time high. As a believer it's clear who defines marriage, and that's God. Divorce is becoming more and more common, with the average marriage lasting twelve years according to an online source[9]. The divorce rate in the United States is nearing 50 percent, meaning half of those who are getting married will have a marriage ending in divorce.[10]

Something a pastor once said stuck with me, "The moment of conversion, your heart became a battleground." And isn't that the truth? I have heard many couples testifying to problems in their life and marriage becoming more amplified since walking with the Lord.

---

[9] I have since read from *The Good News About Marriage* by Shaunti Feldman where she debunks myths about marriage and shares some encouraging statistics. Her research shows the divorce rate has been declining, especially in Christian marriages, the last few years.

[10] Ibid.

It's unwise to enter a battle without proper protection. A quick review: We're not going to win any spiritual battles if we're not fighting with spiritual weapons. I've learned to arm myself against any conflict with the unseen powers of this world by putting on the whole armor of God (Eph. 6:10–18). In conflict, in a marriage, a flurry of angry words or the silent treatment won't cut it.

The Christian life is a war, and attacks are swift from the enemy, especially pertaining to marriage. He hates marriage. How does this *single* girl know this? I know he hates marriage because I have felt and seen him so readily attack this project. I see him attacking marriages too, and it's really what spurred me on even more to get the project going. When anything gets hard, we're tempted to give up, and in most cases we do. Marriage is no different.

Some may choose to end their marriage simply because they've gotten tired. I wish they wouldn't. I wish they'd take the words of the Lord seriously and to heart because I've heard so many times how much blessing awaits on the other side of the hard years. I'm also keenly aware I am one choice away from this as well. We can grow apathetic in our walk with Jesus. As the years wane on, we can forget the ways He woos, we can get weary in the wait, and we can make small compromises that lend to winding us right back to making habitual, poor decisions.

And all along, He had stayed right beside us on the road. We had come so far. But we stop and look back. He pauses ahead and waits. The longing glance back at the thing that no longer serves us is the thing we want most in a moment of weakness. No longer in the honeymoon phase of your relationship with Christ, you're in the character-building middle, and it might seem like, "We're having chicken and potatoes for dinner again?" But it's all on purpose for a purpose when you get to this point with Him. It is not a time to turn back but to persevere and press into Him all the more and remember the moments when you discovered Him as your First Love, to let that motivate you forward.

> In this you rejoice, though now for a little while, if necessary, you have been grieved by various trials, so that the tested genuineness of your faith—more precious than gold that perishes though it is tested by fire—may be found to result in praise and glory and honor at the revelation of Jesus Christ. Though you have not seen him, you love him. Though you do not now see him, you believe in him and rejoice with joy that is inexpressible and filled with glory, obtaining the outcome of your faith, the salvation of your souls (1 Peter 1:5–9, ESV).

No one is above falling or growing so weary they give in to the temptation to take a time-out. This is why I stay so close to God and stay in His Word on the daily. When it comes to marriage, staying close to God is the place to be, especially in those harder middle spots. On this journey, I've learned just how seriously God takes our vows to Him and vows made at the altar on wedding days. Read these verses:

> Here is another thing you do. You cover the LORD'S altar with tears, weeping and groaning because he pays no attention to your offerings and doesn't accept them with pleasure. You cry out, "Why doesn't the LORD accept my worship?" I'll tell you why! Because the LORD witnessed the vows you and your wife made when you were young. But you have been unfaithful to her, though she remained your faithful partner, the wife of your marriage vows. Didn't the LORD make you one with your wife? In body and spirit you are his.

And what does he want? Godly children from your union. So guard your heart; remain loyal to the wife of your youth. "For I hate divorce!" says the LORD, the God of Israel. "To divorce your wife is to overwhelm her with cruelty," says the LORD of Heaven's Armies. "So guard your heart; do not be unfaithful to your wife" (Malachi 2:13–16, NLT).

What powerful, bold words to be heeded!

I feel blessed to come from a home where both my mom and my dad are still living under the same roof and are married. It hasn't always been an easy marriage and they'll be the first ones to tell you that. But I know that I'm among the few who stand under the banner of parents who've stayed together through the trials of life. Growing up, I would look at their wedding album and stare at a photo of their hands one over the other and notice how unweathered their hands look. My mom's hands were so delicate, my dad's, so youthful. I'm sure the day they stood at the altar and recited their vows, they couldn't have imagined what they'd face, who their children would be or become, or anticipate the hardships they'd endure throughout their 35-plus years together.

We always start hopeful and being a wedding photographer, I see that so often displayed in the couples I work with. Why then do so many promising marriages end in divorce? One of the reasons I believe is that many who step before the altar don't fully understand there is an enemy who hates unity, the family and togetherness, and he will be working overtime to make sure to take down this God-defined, God-created union and to pervert it and plot against it no matter the cost.

Something else Rick (from Rick and Michele) said that stuck with me. "When you get married you immediately become public enemy #1 to the enemy. The first thing I tell a couple when they tell me they're going to get married? I talk them out of it. Not because I don't want them to get married, but I want to know why. What are you after? What is the bond here? Have you really hit the real road yet? Because if you haven't, you're going to have a rude awakening."

It's important to build a relationship not on a slippery foundation but on solid rock. "They all lose heart; they come trembling from their strongholds. The LORD lives! Praise be to my Rock! Exalted be God my Savior!" (Ps. 18:45–46, NIV). Jesus even addresses in Matthew the importance of building on a firm foundation:

> Everyone then who hears these words of mine and does them will be like a wise man who built his house on the rock. And the rain fell, and the floods came, and the winds blew and beat on that house, but it did not fall, because it had been founded on the rock. And everyone who hears these words of mine and does not do them will be like a foolish man who built his house on the sand. And the rain fell, and the floods came, and the winds blew and beat against that house, and it fell, and great was the fall of it (Matt. 7:24–27, ESV).

So the question to begin asking is what or who is the Rock to build your life on? For those of us who claim Christ as Lord and Savior, He is the Rock of our salvation, lives, and marriages. We have Him as a starting point for everything, and we build our lives on His Word. The fight against the things that come against marriages is far beyond our scope. Again, it's a spiritual battle, and just like I learned and am still learning, we will need spiritual weapons to withstand the storms and testing that are sure to come. To wrestle against the rulers of this world, the prince of the air, Satan himself, and the influence of culture and the world selling us a completely different narrative—a narrative that is seeking to destroy, dismantle, and break down the definition of a family unit—we will need to faithfully call on the name of the Lord, for He alone has the power to save a marriage and defeat this anti-God agenda. So is this the answer to the high divorce rate? Perhaps it's that many are fighting the wrong battle with the wrong weapons or do not have the right mindset stepping into marriage.

To win the battles, it will take discipline and knowing His Word, reading it daily, praying it back to Him, and looking to Him in all things. He sent His Holy Spirit to dwell within us, to help us in these times of calamity. He brings peace, comfort, and joy in the midst of some of the hardest trials.

A Note on Divorce and Malachi

The Malachi verse I referenced above says God hates divorce and actually states the man who seeks divorce "does violence to the one he should protect" (Mal. 2:16). This is a direct command to the men, to the husbands. It says to "guard your heart" twice. That's an order. By not guarding your heart or your eyes or your mind, you're allowing all sorts of evils in, and it will definitely influence your behavior. This is a stern warning to men who choose not to guard their marriage, wife, and children.

I want to make it known this is not a condemnation against anyone who is divorced or has gone through a divorce. Some things are completely out of our hands. You may have recently found out your husband or wife is being unfaithful. They are showing no sign of repentance for the choices they are making. They actually seem to be getting away with their actions, scot free. You may feel tempted to find vengeance against the persons involved. Can I share one of my favorite verses? "The LORD will fight for you, you need only to be still" (Ex. 14:14, NIV). Fire and lightning bolts come out of that verse when I read it. Give the battle to God. Ask Him to fight on your behalf. The person who's sowing adultery will not walk away unscathed. Know that. When I first read that verse, my heart needed it bad. It made my love for Jesus, the Lord, who is our greatest Defender, grow even more. He was fighting *for* me, I didn't have to do anything.

Again, I don't see this verse as a condemnation but as a declaration and a form of discipleship. As I am writing this book to a young woman, I'd say this is important to note. You want a husband who puts a guard around your heart by guarding his. If it feels hard to wait for the right man right now, remember it will be worth waiting for someone who takes God's Word and His commands seriously. If there's any work to be done on a marriage, it should be done. If it's just that there are feelings of being tired or fed up with your spouse and the spark *feels* like it's out, divorce should not be the ticket out. Vows were made and should be fought to be honored and kept. Biblically, there are no grounds for divorce based on a change of heart or just growing apart. The aforementioned case—the unrepentant, unfaithful spouse or the abusive spouse—is an entirely different story, and the Bible does clarify this is when divorce is acceptable. Or rather, it makes an allowance for it. "Jesus replied, 'Moses permitted divorce only as a concession to your hard hearts, but it was not what God had originally intended. And I tell you this, whoever divorces his wife and marries someone else commits adultery—unless his wife has been unfaithful'" (Matt. 19:8-9, NLT).

> But if the husband or wife who isn't a believer insists on leaving, let them go. In such cases the believing husband or wife is no longer bound to the other, for God has called you

to live in peace. Don't you wives realize that your husbands might be saved because of you? And don't you husbands realize that your wives might be saved because of you? (1 Cor. 7:15–16, NLT).

What Makes Marriage Work?

It's been three years since I launched The Marriage Project. The official launch date was January 23, 2019. I've interviewed over 25 couples and have learned a lot. But the one consistent thing I see is that God blesses God-honoring, God-seeking marriages. Does that mean they're easy? No. One of the couples I've interviewed stated that if you're married to someone who doesn't have a relationship with God, the best thing for you to do would be to get closer to God, to get to know Him better yourself. Get close to Him and begin an amazing adventure with Him, and He'll lead you in ways to pray for your spouse or future spouse.

What brings me great comfort in my season of waiting is the knowledge that Jesus is my Heavenly Husband. That might sound cheesy, but all I really mean by that is that He provides for my every need, protects my heart, and intimately knows me. He knows my greatest desires and listens and loves well. Because He knows me, He knows what's best for me. I've been single for a long time now, but He's held my heart every step of the way.

That is true once you're married too. He will still be your Protector, Provider, and Heavenly Husband. If you find yourself married reading this and you married the person who isn't contributing to helping the marriage work or who doesn't know the Lord, I can say confidently He wants to help you reconcile your marriage and save your family, but first, He wants your heart.

God used a few godly couples in my life to show this girl who only knew unhealthy relationships what to wait for or pray toward. The ultimate purpose of the project is to bring God the glory and to give you a reason to relish in all of who He is and all He's done for us and to cling to what is good and to see that it's Him. I would hope hearing of this God or reminding yourself of who He is would cause you to return to Him as your First Love or discover Him as that for the very first time. It's not marriage or a significant other you need for ultimate satisfaction, it's a right, repentant relationship with Him. That's what love is. Jesus is love.

A guest pastor, Pastor Pancho Jaurez of Calvary Chapel Montebello, spoke one Sunday at my church, and he spoke on the subject of love and marriage, so of course, my ears perked up. I'm fascinated by this subject. He said he's found there are two key things in what it takes to make a marriage work. He said when you stand facing one another at the altar so often you hear the words "I do." The problem with that is perspective. There's this little known fact that humans aren't the best promise keepers when left to doing it without supernatural help. While the intentions of those vows may be right, he said the words at the altar should be something entirely different than the traditional "I do's." He said it'd be more theologically correct if the words were "I die." Because if you haven't caught on, the theme of the Christian life is a death to self, in the same way Christ modeled. Even in marriage we are to die to ourselves. There are at least 34 verses in the Bible that refer to dying to self. Look them up if you have time.

Even with that knowledge, how easy is it to put another's wishes above our own when we want our way? *Not* easy. In today's culture, with people seeking their "best self," many are stepping into marriage hoping to gain something out of it for themselves. The other person is to increase their happiness and contribute to their own success in life.

But the main purpose in marriage was for God to be glorified through it. It is to point to the relationship that Christ has with His Church and to demonstrate love not as a passionate love affair in a harmful way but in a life-giving way. He is the love of a father when your father never told you, "I love you." He places His identity on you. He is the love of a life partner who knows everything about you, chooses you, and loves you purely. He is the example of a self-sacrificial death to self as He took up the cross to save you. He is the model of how to serve one another in love. Love is not just rapturous feelings all of the time. Love is choosing to show up. Love is not self-seeking, it is self-giving. Read what C.S Lewis had to say:

> Being in love is a good thing, but it is not the best thing. There are many things below it, but there are also things above it. You cannot make it the basis of a whole life. It is a noble feeling, but it is still a feeling. Now no feeling can be relied on to last in its full intensity, or even to last at all. Knowledge can last, principles can last, habits can last but feelings come and go. And in fact, whatever people say, the state called "being in love" usually does not last. If the old fairytale ending "They lived happily ever after" is taken to mean "They felt for the next fifty years exactly as they felt the day before they were married," then it says what probably never was nor ever would be true, and would be highly undesirable if it were. Who could bear to live in that excitement for even five years?

> What would become of your work, your appetite, your sleep, your friendships? But, of course, ceasing to be "in love" need not mean ceasing to love. Love in this second sense—love as distinct from "being in love"—is not merely a feeling.

It is a deep unity, maintained by the will and deliberately strengthened by habit; reinforced by in Christian marriages the grace which both partners ask, and receive, from God. They can have this love for each other even at those moments when they do not like each other; as you love yourself even when you do not like yourself. 'Being in love' first moved them to promise fidelity: this quieter love enables them to keep the promise. It is on this love that the engine of marriage is run: being in love was the explosion that started it.

The Altar

Pastor Pancho continued in saying, "There's a reason they call it an altar...because we come to the altar to be altered." But how often is that the focus or the determination by the two standing before the altar? How many truly know this to be true? If we aren't letting Him into our hearts to allow Him to work, then marriage becomes this superficial thing that lacks the mindset of what you're truly to gain from it, which is a preparation for eternity, a molding into the likeness of Christ.

There are many references of altars in the Bible, and they are predominately in the Old Testament. An altar was a place where the blood of an undefiled male goat or lamb would be shed as a sacrifice which provided a temporary covering of sins and foreshadowed the perfect and complete sacrifice of Jesus Christ. Hebrews 9:22 offers us insight into this by stating, "Without the shedding of blood there is no forgiveness." When Jesus came the first time, His sole purpose was for this, to sacrifice Himself so that we may be reconciled back to God and have that walking, talking sort of relationship with Him. We're able to go before a Holy God when we are covered by the blood of the sacrificial Lamb, Jesus Christ. When we follow Him, God's judgment passes over us and His favor rests upon us. The altar at a wedding ceremony can be that moment where we commit to another person and enter into a marriage covenant while it also should be the altar where we lay down our very lives in submission to God's will for our lives.

I was curious to see what the most recent headlines pertaining to marriage at this point in history are and here were some of the top stories: "Why Married Women Keep Secret Bank Accounts," "Money Worries Biggest Reason for Marriages Ending," "National Divorce Day Is Coming," "Singer Pink Opens Up about the Reality of Marriage: 'Monogamy Is Work,'" "Transgender Bride First Ever to Be Formally Married in Nepal," "Groom Asks Guests to Pay for His Wedding."

This is what happens when the world and sinful man is left to their own doing. What I see in each of these is deceit and lies, financial trouble causing marital strife, the admittance that marriage takes intentionality and work, misplaced identity, with a mix of selfishness and confusion to top it off. The main thing is no longer the main thing, its purpose has been lost.

We talked briefly about covenant earlier on, but it is a big deal when understanding how God views marriage, so I thought it important to expound on it a bit more. A marriage covenant is intended by God to be a lifelong, fruitful relationship between a man and a woman. Marriage is a vow to God, to each other, our families, and our community to remain steadfast in unconditional love, reconciliation, and sexual purity, while purposefully growing in our covenant relationship with Him.

An article from Focus on the Family reads, "What woman is as a part of man is not tied to individuated pieces of flesh and bone but is far broader and more profound than that. She is the necessary complement to him that together reveals the glory of the image of God in humanity. Her parts and his parts each have their own order and function. Together and rightly ordered, their united differences ignite the power and glory of creation itself, which is the consummate activity of God from the beginning. So God does a two-stage creation of man."

From *The Divine Marriage*, it reads, "First he makes the full orbed being (Adam, which in the Hebrew means, mankind). Then in phase two, God removes woman from Adam's side and makes Eve, a separate being, though of Adam's substance, designed to ultimately reunite to her source through the mystery of Holy Matrimony." Without covenant, what replaces it is contractual. What is the difference between covenant and contract? This was taken from an online article that no longer has a working link but it was too good not to share. Let's compare:

Contract says: I take thee for me. Covenant says: I give myself to thee.

Contract says: You had better do it. Covenant says: How may I serve you?

Contract says: What do I get? Covenant says: What can I give?

Contract says: I'll meet you halfway. Covenant says: I'll give you 100 percent plus.

Contract says: I have to. Covenant says: I want to.

Marriage is a sacred covenant binding you to another person, not just a piece of paper.

What about that covenant of old, like in Hosea? What the Bible makes clear in Hosea is that Hosea loved Gomer despite all of her shortcomings and adultery. He pleads with her, he tries to stop her leaving, but she insists on returning to her lovers, who offer her material possessions and temporary self-gratification. She would say sorry and come back, Hosea would take her back, forgive her, but then she was shortly back to her old ways, found again with a new lover. No doubt it was because Hosea had experienced God's love and forgiveness that he could extend such love and forgiveness to his wife, and he revered the weight and power of the covenant he had made.

Dear Church

There are numerous mentions of the Church being compared to a bride being readied for her Bridegroom, Jesus Christ. One of those is Revelation 22:17, along with Ephesians 5:25–30. There is a clear call to the Church, as Christ's bride, of what we should be doing while we wait on His return. But are we or are we not like Gomer, chasing after idols of this world?

And so we have it, just as there was a betrothal period in biblical times during which the bride and groom were separated until the wedding, so is the bride of Christ separate from her Bridegroom during the church age. Her responsibility during the betrothal period is to be faithful to Him. There will be a day the church will be united with the Bridegroom and the official "wedding ceremony" will take place and, with it, the eternal union of Christ and His bride will be actualized (Rev. 19:7–9; 21:1–2).

While men are commanded to guard their hearts to protect their wives, as women we must be on guard too. The devil presents half-truths to make it convincing enough to sound like truth and thus keeps us from experiencing God fully. Once our guards are lowered or our egos are heightened, our minds are darkened and much more susceptible to confusion. Even in the garden, Satan saw the woman and decided to strike. His hatred for all things good and pure led him to entice her to join his coalition of insurrection.

What's scary is he is doing the same thing in our world right now in broad daylight. He does this cunningly enough and plays upon human curiosity and sinful nature. He made Eve call into question what God really spoke. The devil knows Scripture, yet he quotes only the parts he wants to twist to sound like truth (Gen. 3:1). Be careful of anything that sounds like truth but is blatantly going against what you know would be honorable to God. "Now the serpent was more crafty than any of the wild animals the LORD God had made. He said to the woman, 'Did God really say, "You must not eat from any tree in the garden"?'" (Gen. 3:1, NIV).

You can choose to get hung up on all sorts of things about woman not being the greatest helpmate for man after this story, but the truth is God's Word is absolute, irrefutable, and it states boldly how God intended companionship- and intimacy-based relationships to be, man and a woman, woman and a man. And knowing this story of Adam and Eve, I see how much of a threat man and woman were together to Satan. I see how much of a threat the *woman* was to Satan. The first time God says something is not good in Genesis is when he states man should not be alone, so He creates Eve and calls them husband and wife.

> Then the LORD God said, "It is not good for the man to be alone. I will make a helper who is just right for him."

> Then the LORD God made a woman from the rib, and he brought her to the man. "At last!" the man exclaimed. This one is bone from my bone, and flesh from my flesh! She will be called 'woman,' because she was taken from 'man.'" This explains why a man leaves his father and mother and is joined to his wife, and the two are united into one. Now the man and his wife were both naked, but they felt no shame (Gen. 2:18, 22–25, NLT).

Thus we must trust this was His good and perfect plan all along.

"The Spirit and the bride say, "Come!"
And let the one who hears say, "Come!"
Let the one who is thirsty come; and let the one who wishes
take the free gift of the water of life."

— Revelation 22:17

Part 3—The Bridegroom and the Wedding Feast

12

As We Wait

"And I saw the holy city, new Jerusalem, coming down out of heaven
from God, made ready as a bride adorned for her husband."
—Revelation 21:2

As the Church, we are awaiting our Bridegroom to return for His Bride. Jesus is returning for His Church, and the day is drawing nearer as evil becomes more rampant. We wait expectantly and like Revelation 22:17 states, "The Spirit and the bride say, 'Come.'" That is an invitation to this future wedding banquet. If you're thirsty, come.

I write and type with wrists and fingers freed by the love of Christ, typing with intentionality, fervor, urgency, and by God's infinite grace to extend the invitation. Ironically, I have begun to consider myself "married" to this project in some ways. It has taken hard work and determination to keep the fire ignited for it. Many other thrills sought to derail my staying faithful to it. Yet here I stand and stay. It's had its own financial hard times. I've learned the importance of communication because of it and have learned how to make decisions through this process. I've remained true to its message even when doubt coaxed me to throw in the towel and leave it behind. I stand by it and vow to see it to completion because

I believe in its message, I believe in what God has imparted to me. There have been rays of sunlight and victory, which beamed through the more menial task of writing.

And since the writing of this all, God has done a mighty work through this project. I have to tell one last story. The same year the project launched, God took me to South Africa to record with a couple that He used majorly in my life in that pivotal 2013 year.

I could go into all the details of how much God had to work out to even get me on a plane to fly by myself to the African continent, but I'll spare you. Let's just say, He did it. I never imagined in a million years, the girl who went from bar hopping to shyly sitting in the back of a Bible study, who barely made it through her first mission trip experience would fly 23-plus hours to record with a couple I'd only ever admired and not yet personally met. The plan was to stay with a dear friend's mom in Cape Town and fly to Jeffery's Bay to stay a few nights with Vanessa and Rehgert Vanzyl, the couple I interviewed and recorded with in South Africa, who wisely shared with us a bit more about covenant and commitment.

This couple was so epochal because God used them at the end of 2013 to show me what a husband who honors Christ as Lord first and who honors his wife second looks like. The event was a fundraiser hosted by their organization called Aleph Surf International. Rehgert is South African, Vanessa is from California. I didn't know that at the time or any part of their story because Vanessa did not speak from the stage that night but Rehgert's accent gave his background away.

The purpose of Aleph Surf International is restoration through recreation meaning giving youth and their families opportunities they may never have otherwise. Through surf lessons, Rehgert builds relationships with the local girls and boys, which cultivates child-development and in turn produces confident, purpose-filled youth.

This in turn produces community leaders later. Vanessa contributes by using her fashion background and expertise by creating and designing clothing pieces to fundraise while giving jobs to the local community, mainly women. But most importantly, these youth are mentored and learn about the God who created them. Aleph is the first letter of the Hebrew alphabet, and it symbolizes the beginning or foundation of something. Through their ministry, Aleph helps lay a strong foundation rooted in Christ.

After the podcast launched in January, it seemed like the time to begin reaching out to more prospective couples to interview. I remembered Vanessa and Rehgert and wondered how I could even begin to express how I'd even come to know who they were and pitch the idea of the project. Banking on God's faithfulness I just went for it and knew if it was His will for me to go visit them, He would send me.

Vanessa's response back to me, once again, blew me away. She invited me to come to South Africa and said they would love to host me. She went even further in saying some very beautiful and profound things about God's heart for marriage and just how important it was for the Church to be ready for her Bridegroom's near arrival to collect his Bride. Tickets were booked, plans were made, and my two week South African adventure commenced.

Going across the world alone seemed challenging, but I knew God was with me. He spoke this promise to me, "And he said, 'My presence will go with you, and I will give you rest'" (Ex. 33:14, ESV). My host family in Cape Town were amazing and took excellent care of me. They were my home base. Two days after I arrived in Cape Town, I had to travel back to the airport to get on another one-hour flight to the Eastern Cape, where Vanessa and Rehgert would pick me up. As I sat on a small plane flying over the southernmost point of Africa, a striking thought hit me. I was bringing the fight back to the enemy. That's how much God's heart was moved on the matter. He would take such great measures to get me to this point. A surge of purpose pulsed through my veins.

Getting off the plane and walking through the Port Elizabeth airport was even more surreal, and seeing Vanessa and Rehgert in person after six years of getting a brief glimpse into their marriage was even more so. Their kind hearts and arms swept me up, and we began the drive an hour back to their home. As we drove, they began to unpack their story for me. As we recorded, they shared so beautifully on the Father's heart and God's covenant promise to His people. Vanessa highlighted the specifics of their wedding ceremony and how present God was in all the details. It made me think longer on the wedding day and specifically the wedding feast, which Jesus says He is preparing right now for His bride when He returns for us. It's mind-blowing really, that the Bible uses the wedding, marriage, a bride and bridegroom, and the wedding feast as the picture of redemption, restoration, gathering, and intimacy.

And yet so many miss it, and we don't think about why we do what we do. What is the meaning behind the ceremony and celebration and why do we value marriage? Why do we do what we do? Here is the answer—like everything else we do, it points us to Christ. The wedding feast and marriage and all the hoopla surrounding the union of man and woman points to the trinity, God the Father, the Son, and Holy Spirit, and He's inviting everyone to the Marriage Supper of the Lamb. God does not wish that anyone should perish without being made right with Him (1 Tim. 1:1–5). As He opens our heart to Him, we understand verses like this:

> Then I heard again what sounded like the shout of a vast crowd or the roar of mighty ocean waves or the crash of loud thunder: "Praise the Lord!"

For the LORD our God, the Almighty, reigns.

Let us be glad and rejoice,
and let us give honor to him.

For the time has come for the wedding feast of the Lamb,
and his bride has prepared herself.

She has been given the finest of pure white linen to wear.

For the fine linen represents the good deeds of God's
holy people.

And the angel said to me, "Write this: Blessed are those
who are invited to the wedding feast of the Lamb." And he
added, "These are true words that come from God" (Rev.
19:6–9, NLT).

Jesus tells a parable of a wedding feast in Matthew 22. This once
again points to Jesus's invitation to receive God's free gift of salvation
through Himself and points to Israel's continued rejection of God's
offered inheritance promised through Abraham's descendants. Just
like Hosea was sent to warn the people, many other prophets were
sent to warn the people that they had turned their hearts to idols
and false gods and to repent.

The prophets were sent to warn of punishment for their continued rejection of God and to point forward to Christ so they
would know Him as Messiah when He came. When Jesus did come,
as God spoke and promised, most did not receive Him, but instead
they sent Him to the cross because He wasn't what they were waiting
for. To this day there are some Jews who continue to reject Him as

Messiah. They wanted a king who would free them from the Roman rule, but He first came to save them and free them from a bondage greater than a pagan king and nation.

In the parable of the wedding feast, this invitation is compared to being invited to a royal wedding banquet, yet the many who were invited came up with a number of excuses and declined the invitation offered to them, illustrating the Jews refusal to repent of their rebellion against God. God then turned and offered His gift of salvation and inheritance to the Kingdom of Heaven to the Gentiles (non-Jews), and we were grafted in.

In the parable of the wedding feast, just as the king provides wedding garments for those not properly dressed for the occasion, He provides salvation to those outside the initial promised inheritance. The wedding hall would be empty as the Jews continued on in their rejection of his invitation, yet it is now full with guests who've been invited and have accepted, Christians who believe in Christ as Lord (a diverse bunch who come from all different cultures and backgrounds) and some Messianic Jews, who have turned to Christ and acknowledge Him as Lord.

More revelation has come to me about the wedding feast at weddings I've photographed that tied in with another thought as I was leaving South Africa and saying the hard goodbyes to strangers turned friends turned family in Christ. What's so special about a wedding reception and weddings is that all your people are together in one place. You invite them to come together and rejoice in this union. It is beautifully decorated, and it brings such joy to have all your loved ones around you. To think how beautiful the reception that Jesus is preparing right now, the most beautiful banquet (Isa. 25:6–8), for the most glorious union, Christ and His Church.

Then, I had this vision of all of us believers all together, gathered, like the sweetness of all your people together on your wedding day. I saw a glimpse of this once before as heaven met earth in the summer of 2016. I went to Washington, DC, with friends to attend a conference where many Christian leaders, pastors, and worship artists came together to call on the name of Jesus and *be* the church. The intent was to gather one million Christians on the mall in DC to pray for our nation. The plan was to listen to different speakers throughout the day, with time to stop and pray together in corporate prayer with worship mixed in. The lineup of speakers and worship artists was exciting.

It was an extremely hot, humid day, but then the rain came. Because of the sudden torrential downpour, the event was cut short. The event was supposed to go late into the night, but God had other, better plans. Many ran for cover, others stayed out in the rain praying. We were among the ones walking to our car to get to a friend's house to take refuge. The emphasis I wanted to make and why I even share this story is twofold. I saw the church be the church that day. As we were moving out in crowds, believers were stopping to talk to a homeless man and pray with him, believers who didn't know each other before that moment stopped to pray together in prayer circles at the corner of a crosswalk. Prayer was happening all over the city. It was amazing.

The rain couldn't stop what God wanted to do. And instead of staying in our Christian bubble on the mall, He sent us out. The Spirit of God was moving among us all, and many were introduced to Jesus that weekend because of what He was leading us all to do. The other reason I share this story here is because of the beauty I saw as so many gathered together worshipping the Lord—it made me think of Heaven. To think of all of your people, or everyone of us who believes like that together doing that very thing in eternity, gathered together under the banner of His love makes me want to invite more people to know Jesus, to be brought into this loving company of people who love Him with all their heart, soul, strength, and mind.

As the rain stopped about an hour later, a double rainbow shone through the sky, a symbol of God's covenant promise to His people. He also sent a rainbow over the house I stayed at in Cape Town. Another reminder of His covenant promise. I went to church the second Sunday I was in South Africa, and we sang a song during worship that sang, "For endless days we will sing Your praise, O Lord, O Lord, our God." Endless days. *Endless.* That hit me because how much melancholy do we feel after a gathering comes to an end? The anticipation is gone, and all your people disperse. The fullness of joy in having all the people you love in one place has an end. Until one day, the endless days, where we won't ever have to say goodbye, and we'll all be together. We can look forward to being in His presence forever, with those who've been saved and believe in Him, and we'll enjoy the wedding feast and celebration that won't ever end. We get to bask in the glory of His presence, together, for eternity, feasting on His love and provision and goodness. No more sin, no more heartbreak, no more emptiness. And until then, in the melancholy place of waiting for the next reunion or the next hug from a loved one, we are left only with Him, and what a glorious spot to be, in the company of our Bridegroom, Jesus. He will delicately hold our heart until *that* day.

I believe wholeheartedly He's seen you holding this book all along, and it's not by accident that you've picked it up. He created a guest list of readers long before the words were ever revealed to me, and He knew you'd need its message for such a time as this. Whether you're single and hurting, whether you're in a relationship giving your body over and over to a person who does not have the ability to care for your heart and continues to hurt you, whether you're married and have hit a crisis in that marriage, or whether you've walked away from the church and are living in a lifestyle you know goes against God's Word—this has been waiting for you, to heal your heart and bring you back to a place of communion with God. He's busting down doors to come and get you and bring you back to a place of safety and fellowship with Him through Christ Jesus. He's calling to you. "Again, the Spirit and the bride say, 'Come.' Let anyone who hears this say, 'Come.' Let anyone who is thirsty come. Let anyone who desires drink freely from the water of life" (Rev. 22:17, NLT).

Vanessa shared in their episode about her wedding day and that she had her bridesmaids walk down the aisle with oil lamps symbolizing another parable, the Parable of The Ten Virgins, in the Bible:

Then the kingdom of heaven will be comparable to ten virgins, who took their lamps and went out to meet the groom. Five of them were foolish, and five were prudent. For when the foolish took their lamps, they did not take extra oil with them; but the prudent took oil in flasks along with their lamps.

Now while the groom was delaying, they all became drowsy and began to sleep. But at midnight there finally was a shout, "Behold, the groom! Come out to meet him." Then all those virgins got up and trimmed their lamps. But the foolish virgins said to the prudent ones, "Give us some of your oil, for our lamps are going out."

However, the prudent ones answered, "No, there most certainly would not be enough for us and you too; go instead to the merchants and buy some for yourselves." But while they were on their way to buy the oil, the groom came, and those who were ready went in with him to the wedding feast; and the door was shut. Yet later, the other virgins also came, saying, "Lord, lord, open up for us." But he answered, "Truly I say to you, I do not know you" (Matt. 25:1–12, NASB).

This is simply posing a question to our hearts: Are our oil lamps filled or empty? Are we ready for His return or have we gone away and risk Him returning while we've gone away? If you've read this far and are thinking, "I am sold. I am tired of feeling empty and alone. I want Jesus in my life, and I want to claim Him as my First Love and know Him as my Bridegroom," it takes a simple confession and a prayer to receive Him into your heart, declaring your belief in Him. I think the biggest hurdle to get over is confessing. How can we be in open, honest communication with someone if we aren't going to bring the things we are more comfortable hiding to the light? We've learned the value in that together through these pages. It starts there. And it continues with a genuine choice to ask Him to help you daily turn from those things that tempt to throw you off course, just like He helped me and the others who are a part of the podcast.

Jesus is Love

Love isn't just a slogan that declares "it wins." It isn't what Hollywood tells you it is. Love has a name, and His name is Jesus Christ. His love casts out all fear (1 Jn. 4:18). It's not all talk and no action, His love takes action. True Love gives, it vows, it commits, it shows up, and it is self-sacrificing. It demonstrates to a lost world a holy God and reveals a rebellious sinner who needs forgiveness.

True Love is patient, it is kind, it does not demand its own way, keeps no record of wrong (1 Cor. 13:4–8) and true love covers...a multitude of sins (1 Pet. 4:8). His love and blood cover us. It stills us. He quiets us with His love. No more shouting matches, no more covering up bruises from pounding on doors from that fight. His perfect love casts out all fear: fear of abandonment, fear of unfaithfulness, fear of failure, fear of flying across the world alone. He casts it out. He will never leave you nor forsake you (Deut. 31:6). He is true to His Word.

His love persists. His love wiped away my tears, and He showed me where perfect love is found. It's found in Him and in His Word. He wants you to know this type of love. He wants to bring purpose to you in singleness. He wants to restore your health and heal you from disease and the choices you've been making. He wants to protect your heart and will safeguard it. He wants you living in purity and bringing your every need and struggle to Him. He requires death to self and will help you through the more harrowing days. He may want to bring you a marriage that will glorify Him through it, or He may call you to celibacy and singleness. That might sound extreme, but it's all so that He can sew you up and use your story to tell His story. He knows how badly you want your marriage to turn around or how desperately you want your husband to believe in Jesus so that you can do Kingdom work together and fight those spiritual battles together in prayer. He sees. He knows. But first, He wants His rightful place on the throne of your heart.

He is a real-life knight in shining armor who will one day ride in on a horse coming for His bride. It's true.

Now I saw heaven opened, and behold, a white horse.

And He who sat on him *was* called Faithful and True,
    and in righteousness He judges and makes war.

His eyes *were* like a flame of fire, and on His head *were* many crowns.

He had a name written that no one knew except Himself.

He *was* clothed with a robe dipped in blood, and His name is called The Word of God.

And the armies in heaven, clothed in fine linen, white and clean, followed Him on white horses.

Now out of His mouth goes a sharp sword, that with it He should strike the nations.

And He Himself will rule them with a rod of iron.

He Himself treads the winepress of the fierceness and wrath of Almighty God.

And He has on *His* robe and on His thigh a name written:

KING OF KINGS AND LORD OF LORDS.

—Revelation 19:11–16, NKJV

His love covered Adam and Eve's shame (Gen. 3:7, 21). There is no sin so great that God's love doesn't cover. So are you ready? If you feel in your heart you are wanting to receive His covering, His free gift of salvation, and you are ready to flee from that thing or person that's causing unrest in your soul and you want to turn to Jesus in repentance, now is the time. Today is the day of salvation

(2 Cor. 6:2). It would be my honor to lead you in that and figuratively hold your hands and pray with you. This is if you're ready to relinquish *your* will, wanting to hand over anything that you've allowed in your life that's become an idol or has taken the place of God in your heart and life.

I pray you feel your pride melting away in this moment, that your heart is softening to the message of Jesus Christ, and that the sharing of His Word has illuminated the darkened parts of your heart (Ps. 119:105; Ephes. 4:18). If you're ready, pray out loud or in your heart now.

Lord Jesus,

I know I'm a sinner, but I know You're the Savior. I believe You died for my sin and rose from the grave so that I may have eternal life in You. I confess my pride and rebellion. I confess that I've forged on in my own way ignoring Your countless attempts to pull me out of the dark, bottomless pit my choices have put me in. I've allowed people or things into my life and heart that have taken Your rightful place. I've made a mess of my life.

I want to call you Lord and know You as that. I want You to come into my life now. You're my only hope, and I need you to resuscitate me to life. I turn from my sin now and choose to follow You, no matter the cost because I now understand what it cost You, Your very life. I give You permission to extract the things out of my life that are causing more harm than good. It may be painful in the moment, but I trust You. Keep me from desiring to go back to those places I know I should not go and help me to see the light of the truth of Your Word. Thank You for loving me with this pure, unadulterated love. Thank You for choosing me and offering me this free gift of salvation, thank You for forgiving my sin and for the promise of eternity spent with You. In Your beautiful name, I pray. Amen.

If you've prayed that, welcome to the family of God! And welcome to the best kind of love you'll ever experience. Welcome to a life fulfilled, a life with purpose and eternity promised. You may not have felt anything in that moment, but I highly encourage you to get a Bible, get into your Word daily, and begin on this amazing journey with Jesus, our Bridegroom, who one day will be returning for His bride.

I pray you begin to experience the kind of love that 1 Corinthians 13 speaks about, a love that bears all, does not envy or boast, is not proud, not self-seeking, not easily angered, rejoices with the truth, always protects, hopes, perseveres, and never fails. This love covers the offense of an offender to preserve a friendship, a relationship — *that* is love. It knows you, *all* of you and yet still loves you. He loves you enough to not let you stay the same. His love will change you from the inside out, through His Holy Word for the better and for the Kingdom. His love chose you (Jn. 15:16). No more covering up shame or guilt. No more lying. Just resting and leaning on your Beloved, Christ, who bore the shame and guilt for all. For His love, His bride. A love that covers. I'm so thankful for Him and to be His.

As we wait, let us be found faithful and serving Him with all of our hearts, all of our minds, all of our strength, and all of our soul.

And see you at the wedding feast, I sincerely hope.

Author's Note

I have referenced different translations of the Bible throughout this book. I have found throughout different seasons of walking with God, He spoke to me through a number of different translations, and this is why I shared from so many of them. These were verses He used to speak to me in different seasons, and I thought it'd be fitting to share that as you walked through a few pivotal years of my story with me, the part where I was learning to read and value the Bible. My two favorites and the most thorough holding it up to the original Aramaic/Hebrew text of the Scriptures are the ESV (English Standard Version) and NKJV (New King James Version). When I want to challenge myself, I'll grab my KJV (King James Version) Bible and do my best to decipher the way things are worded. I only had one Bible when I first began reading God's Word and studying it. But then I grabbed my mom's Life Application Study Bible and immersed myself in the chapter outlines, verse breakdowns, and historical/cultural facts. Now I have several, and one of my most cherished is *The Complete Jewish Study Bible*. I can read the names from the original language, and it opens up an entirely new layer of God's Word I'd never discovered before.

When I study the Word, I like to have my one main study Bible, physically in front of me. There is nothing like holding the Word of God in tangible form. You can highlight things, underline, circle, and take side notes as you uncover the truth and treasure of God's Word. While it's easy to pull up the Bible on an app on your phone, your phone is also a very distracting place. Plus, there's just nothing like flipping the pages of a book, holding the spine, and reading off something that isn't shining more blue light into your eyes. I'd suggest purchasing your first Bible if you've never purchased one before or go dust the one you have off sitting in your bookshelf.

The ESV Study Bible would be a great place to start. Or some other recommendations are *The One Year Bible* (takes you through the entire Bible in a year), *The Life Application Study Bible*, or a Journaling Bible (just make sure you have a reliable translation such as ESV, NIV, AMP, NLT, NKJV).

God's Word is like oxygen to me. It is a lifeline. It keeps me grounded, it refreshes me, and helps me make daily decisions. It is a great discipline to work into your morning routine. It gets the day started on the right note, connecting with the Creator of the universe, who is infinitely wise and infinitely generous with extending His wisdom and mercy to us.

If you're not sure where to start, begin in the Psalms or the book of John. You will read from King David's heart and pen throughout the Psalms and read one of the four gospels, real-life eyewitness accounts testifying to Jesus' life, ministry, death, and resurrection. I encourage you to find a good Bible study to join, making sure the group or church studies the Bible in all its entirety, not just the New Testament and not just an author's book. If it were the latter, that would be more of a book club, which is fine too, but it does not replace the study of God's Word.

I wish we could study together, but we'll be learning and discovering the truth of God's Word together in spirit.

Closing Thoughts

I hope this book and project can serve as a blueprint to the coming generations and for the church—to uphold God's standard in families and in marriages no matter what the culture or world is telling you. And the reminder that first we are married to God, then to the one He's given us in marriage. That is, if He decides marriage to be part of our individual story. One woman. One man. I want to leave you with the reminder of the greatest love story ever told, Jesus' love for His bride and to take a moment and think on His love—Jesus loves perfectly. He's never uttered a word He hasn't intended to fulfill. To experience marriage in the way that I always dreamed of experiencing it is going to take a holy God to bring two broken people together, wholly consecrated to Him. This is the only way to make any sort of relationship last and work.

"For the LORD God is a sun and shield;
The LORD bestows favor and honor;
No good thing will He withhold from those who walk
uprightly" (Ps. 84:11, ESV).

Claim that promise! No good thing will He withhold from those who walk uprightly. And no matter the battles we face in this life we can rest assured that the victory is His! The war is already won.

And God gives us tools as we fight for the things worth fighting for this side of Heaven—our marriages, our children, our homes, our relationship with Him. This fallen state isn't how He intended it to be. We were never meant to have broken communion with Him, broken relationships, insecurities, jealousies, pride, or shame. We were never meant to be trapped in a world with sin, death, and decay. But that's the reality we face. We know the story of Adam and Eve. Eve was tempted, and she took the bait. Let's be really honest with ourselves and just fully own that we would have done the same thing. It's easy to point the finger at Eve, but I've had many Eve moments where I listen to the lies of the enemy and take the bite.

> "But I am afraid that just as Eve was deceived by the serpent's cunning, your minds may somehow be led astray from your sincere and pure devotion to Christ" (2 Cor. 11:3, NIV).

As God has picked up the broken pieces of my story, there have been amazing breakthroughs in my heart and mind and incredible moments that I couldn't have planned in my wildest of wild dream planners. There are stories that I couldn't make up even if I tried. And there's proof to that because I did try to write the script to my life. There was nothing awe-striking about it. My story really began when I decided to recommit my life to Christ and invited Jesus to be my personal Lord and Savior, the *Author* and Finisher of my faith. My story before inviting Jesus to live in my heart would predominately be about haphazard mistakes and the "what not to do's" in life and relationships.

It's amazing what begins to happen when we humble ourselves before a Mighty God. Pride told me I knew better than God and that I could do life my own way, in my own timing, and I left God out of the equation. In the devotional *My Utmost for His Highest*, Oswald Chambers says, "Pride is an all around evil. It was through pride that the devil became the devil. Pride leads to every other vice. It is the complete anti-God state of mind."

The devil doesn't look like a red-suited demon with a pitchfork and pointy tail. He is the thing that will feed your ego the most or that will distract you from God and cause your mind to be depraved, feeding off our sinful state. If you do things God's way, He will bring you the desires of your heart (Ps. 37:4). He will *give* you the desires of your heart, as in He will literally place new desires there because you begin desiring the things of God as you fall deeper and deeper in love with Him. When you experience Him fully, your heart can't help but delight in Him. He plants new desires because He knows what He has in store for you. I believe He has an amazing husband for me, and He's preparing an amazing marriage for us, but the key to that is God. I've had to "dare to hope" for that because it hasn't come quite as quick as I would have imagined or wanted it to come. But waiting for God's best and doing the tasks in front of me first and letting healing settle in before is definitely all the Lord's doing. To have any sort of marriage that will stand against the wiles of the devil, we need to be equally yoked (2 Cor. 6:14), and I will wait for that man because it's worth it. Just as I stand on the rock of Christ, so will he. We will be in the war together and must be ready to fight this spiritual battle with spiritual weapons, together.

God spoke to me that I shouldn't remove any jewels from my crown, that He has a man strong enough to carry mine, meaning I should not become less of who I am in Christ just because loneliness may creep in time and again. No, I believe He has the best for me, and I will wait for that story and testimony, and I can be doing things for Him while I wait. It's important to not bind yourself to someone who is not fit for you.

"Do not be unequally bound together with unbelievers [do not make mismatched alliances with them, inconsistent with your faith]. For what partnership can righteousness have with lawlessness? Or what fellowship can light have with darkness?" (2 Cor. 6:14, AMP).

Light and darkness have no business being together, let alone married together. Single ladies, be careful who you attach yourself to. Look to the only One who is faithful and true. Two of the most desirable things in a marriage are faithfulness and trustworthiness. Jesus is those things! No matter who comes in and seems like they're there to save the day, if that man or woman is not in love with Jesus, they don't have the ability, in their own strength, to love you wholly, completely. If you're single, spend your time getting more acquainted with your Heavenly Father and discovering what you like to do. Hold on for the one who will complement you and trust that God knows who that is. Let Him find them for you. And serve Him while you wait. And when someone does enter the picture, ask the Lord to show you if their faith is genuine. Are they ready to lead you into His love more and more? See how Jesus pursues, like a gentleman, and find a man like that. As His love pursued me, He's pursuing you.

God bless you and keep you and make His face shine upon you! (Num. 6:23-25)

Because I love Zion,
I will not keep still.
Because my heart yearns for Jerusalem,
I cannot remain silent.
I will not stop praying for her
until her righteousness shines like the dawn,
and her salvation blazes like a burning torch.

The nations will see your righteousness.
World leaders will be blinded by your glory.
And you will be given a new name
by the Lord's own mouth.

The Lord will hold you in his hand for all to see—
a splendid crown in the hand of God.

Never again will you be called "The Forsaken City"
or "The Desolate Land."
Your new name will be "The City of God's Delight"
and "The Bride of God,"
for the Lord delights in you
and will claim you as his bride.

— Isaiah 62:1–4

Endnotes

Batterson, Mark. *The Circle Maker: Praying Circles Around Your Biggest Dreams and Greatest Fears.* Grand Rapids, Michigan: Zondervan. 2016.

Bounds, E.M. *Power Through Prayer.* Whitaker House. 1982.

Chambers, Oswald. *My Utmost for His Highest.* Barbour Books. 1783.

Elliot, Elisabeth. *Passion and Purity: Learning to Bring Your Love Life Under Christ's Control.* Grand Rapids, Michigan: Revell. 1984, 2002.

Foster, David Kyle, *"The Divine Order to Marriage." Focus on the Family.* http://www.focusonthefamily.com/marriage/gods-design-for-marriage/marriage-gods-idea/the-divine-order-to-marriage. — *The Divine Marriage: God's Purpose & Design for Human Sexuality.* 2020.

Henry, Matthew. *Psalms 63. Bible Study Tools.* Accessed February 26, 2021. https://www.biblestudytools.com/commentaries/matthew-henry-complete/psalms/63. html.

———*Song of Solomon 8. Bible Study Tools* .https://www.biblestudytools.com/commentaries/matthew-henry-complete/song-of-solomon/song-of-solomon-8. html.

———*Jeremiah 17. Bible Study Tools.* https: //www.biblestudytools.com/commentaries/matthew-henry-complete/jeremiah/17. html.

Hosie, Rachel. *Divorce Day: January 8 Most Popular Day to Start Legal Proceedings to Dissolve Marriages. Independent.* https: // www.independent.co.uk/lifestyle/love-sex/divorce-day-date-january-8-marriage-end-start-legal-proceedings-most-popular-lawyers-solicitors-a8139251. html.

Lewis, C.S. *The Weight of Glory*. New York, NY. Harper Collins, 1980

————*Mere Christianity*. HarperOne. 2009.

Murray, Andrew. *Humility: The Journey Toward Holiness*. Bloomington, MN. Bethany House Publishers, 2001.

Pounds, Wil. "Exodus 26:31–35; Hebrews 10:19–22 The Veil in the Tabernacle." *Christ in the Old Testament*. http: //www.abideinchrist. com/messages/ex26v31. html.

Robinson, Phil and Jones, Colin. "Why did Jesus Wear a Crown of Thorns?" 2016. https://creation.com/why-did-jesus-wear-a-crown-of-thorns

Siskin, Joshua. *Jerusalem Roses*. 2016. http: //thesmartergardener.com/ jerusalem-roses/.

Torrey, R.A. *The Power of Prayer*. Zondervan. 1987.

——— *How to Obtain Fullness of Power*. Sword of the Lord. 2000.

Author unknown. "What Is A Marriage Covenant?" *Covenant Marriage Movement,* 2017, http: //covenantmarriage.com/what-is-a-marriage-covenant/

Triller, Kaeley. "Bathroom Rules Must Protect, Not Enable." 2017. https:// decisionmagazine.com/bathroom-rules-mustprotect-not-enable-2/

**Stay connected and listen
to the stories of the project/podcast —**

Website: www.themarriageproject.co
Instagram: @themarriageprojectco
Facebook Page: The Marriage Project Co.

The podcast is found on all major podcast sites,
Apple Podcasts, Google Play, & Spotify.
Search "The Marriage Project."

More writing and work from the author can be found at:

Website: www.alyshamiller.com
Instagram: @alysha.miller
www.alyshamiller.com/blog

CPSIA information can be obtained
at www.ICGtesting.com
Printed in the USA
FSHW010153181121
86234FS